Library Technology
REPORTS
Expert Guides to Library Systems and Services

E-book Platforms for Libraries

Mirela Roncevic

ALA TechSource
alatechsource.org

American Library Association

Library Technology REPORTS

ALA TechSource purchases fund advocacy, awareness, and accreditation programs for library professionals worldwide.

Volume 49, Number 3
E-book Platforms for Libraries

ISBNs: (print) 978-0-8389-5888-9; (PDF) 978-0-8389-5889-6; (ePub) 978-0-8389-5890-2; (Kindle) 978-0-8389-5891-9.

American Library Association
50 East Huron St.
Chicago, IL 60611-2795 USA
alatechsource.org
800-545-2433, ext. 4299
312-944-6780
312-280-5275 (fax)

Advertising Representative
Patrick Hogan
phogan@ala.org
312-280-3240

Editor
Patrick Hogan
phogan@ala.org
312-280-3240

Copy Editor
Judith Lauber

Production and Design
Tim Clifford, Production Editor
Karen Sheets de Gracia, Manager of Design and Composition

Library Technology Reports (ISSN 0024-2586) is published eight times a year (January, March, April, June, July, September, October, and December) by American Library Association, 50 E. Huron St., Chicago, IL 60611. It is managed by ALA TechSource, a unit of the publishing department of ALA. Periodical postage paid at Chicago, Illinois, and at additional mailing offices. POSTMASTER: Send address changes to Library Technology Reports, 50 E. Huron St., Chicago, IL 60611.

Trademarked names appear in the text of this journal. Rather than identify or insert a trademark symbol at the appearance of each name, the authors and the American Library Association state that the names are used for editorial purposes exclusively, to the ultimate benefit of the owners of the trademarks. There is absolutely no intention of infringement on the rights of the trademark owners.

ALA TechSource
alatechsource.org

Copyright © 2013 Mirela Roncevic
All Rights Reserved.

About the Author

Mirela Roncevic is an independent content developer, editor, and writer recognized for spearheading a number of initiatives in the LIS field, including the overhaul of reference coverage in *Library Journal* and the magazine's first e-book reviews column. She is co-editor of ALA's *eContent Quarterly* journal as well as consultant to e-content producers, including publishers and library vendors. She has also managed publications of LIS books and newsletters and developed free online resources for librarians, including the Library Grants Center and the Library Blog Directory. In addition, she edited Neal-Schuman's 2009 title *Library Journal Guide to E-Reference Resources*. Roncevic is also a contributor to several online outlets, including *No Shelf Required*, where she posts opinion pieces on digital publishing and e-content development. Follow her on Twitter @MirelaRoncevic.

Abstract

Library Technology Reports (vol. 49, no. 3) "E-book Platforms for Libraries" provides an overview of the various types of e-book platforms available to academic, research, public, and K–12 libraries in the United States (and beyond). The focus is on the products that house electronic versions of books also available in print. A directory lists platforms and identifies the type of platform, e-books, subject areas, and library market; main subject areas; and business models. Four summary tables help readers compare options.

Get Your *Library Technology Reports* Online!

Subscribers to ALA TechSource's *Library Technology Reports* can read digital versions, in PDF and HTML formats, through the scholarly content host MetaPress. Subscribers also have access to an archive of past issues. Visit alatechsource.metapress.com to begin reading. Beside each issue title you will see a solid green box indicating that it is available to you. You may need to log in to be recognized by the system. Please contact MetaPress Support, support@metapress.com, if you have any questions about or problems with access.

Subscriptions
alatechsource.org/subscribe

Contents

Chapter 1—Introduction   5
    Marketplace Basics   6
    Publisher E-book Platforms   6
    Aggregator E-book Platforms   7
    Distributors and E-book Lending Services   7
    University Press Consortium E-book Platforms   8
    E-book Platforms in Academic and Research Libraries   8
    E-book Platforms in Public Libraries   8
    E-book Platforms in K–12 and School Libraries   9

Chapter 2—Criteria for Purchasing E-book Platforms   10
    Content   10
    Technical Specifications   11
    Functionality   11
    Business Models   12

Chapter 3—Directory of E-book Platforms for Libraries   14
    123Library   14
    3M Cloud Library   15
    ABC-CLIO eBook Collection   15
    Axis 360   15
    Books24x7   16
    Books at JSTOR   16
    Books@Ovid   16
    Brain Hive   17
    Cambridge Books Online (CBO)   17
    dawsonera   17
    De Gruyter Online   18
    EBL (Ebook Library)   18
    eBooks on EBSCOhost   18
    ebrary   19
    epointbooks.com   19
    Follett eBooks   19
    Freading Ebook Service   20
    FreedomFlix   20
    Gale Virtual Reference Library (GVRL)   21
    Infobase eBooks   21
    Knovel   21
    LexisNexis Digital Library   22
    Literati by Credo   22
    MackinVIA   22
    McGraw-Hill eBook Library   23
    MyiLibrary   23

Contents, continued

OverDrive	23
Oxford Handbooks Online	24
Oxford Reference	24
Palgrave Connect	24
PsycBOOKS	25
Questia	25
R2 Digital Library	26
Routledge Reference Online	26
Safari Books Online	26
SAGE Knowledge	27
ScienceDirect	27
Sharpe Online Reference (SOLR)	27
SpringerLink	28
SpringerReference	28
StarWalk Kids Media	28
Storia	29
SwetsWise	29
Taylor & Francis eBooks	29
TrueFlix	30
University Press Scholarship Online (UPSO)	30
University Publishing Online	31
UPCC Book Collections on Project MUSE	31
Wheelers ePlatform	31
Wiley Online Library	31
World Book Web	32

Chapter 4—E-book Platforms for Libraries   33

Table 4.1—At-a-glance overview of fifty-one e-book platforms	34
Table 4.2.1—Comparative overview of thirty-five e-book platforms—content and technical specifications	35
Table 4.2.2—Comparative overview of thirty-five e-book platforms—functionality	38
Table 4.2.3—Comparative overview of thirty-five e-book platforms—business model details	40

Chapter 1

Introduction

Abstract

Chapter 1 of Library Technology Reports *(vol. 49, no. 3) "E-book Platforms for Libraries" provides an explanation of the different types of for-fee platforms that have emerged in the e-book market in recent years, including those produced by publishers, aggregators, and distributors, and also by various technology companies with little or no background in the book business prior to the e-revolution. This chapter also touches on the unique needs of librarians purchasing e-books in public, academic, and K–12 settings.*

Librarians are inundated with the choices available to them when selecting e-book platforms for their institutions. Some platforms serve primarily as tools for lending e-books to patrons; others serve as research tools for students and faculty. Some are available directly from publishers who curate the content; others come from aggregators and distributors who amass content from disparate sources. Some provide broad coverage of subjects and are suitable for all libraries; others have scholarly undertones, target niche markets with subject-specific content, and may be of interest only to certain types of institutions.

Not only do librarians and information professionals need to keep up with the proliferation of e-book platforms, they need to keep up with how those they already have access to are evolving. As library vendors continue to experiment with business models, consolidate content, and merge with competitors, librarians need help figuring out how to sort through the myriad options and choose what to purchase based on the needs of the institutions they serve. Many things come into play, with pricing and access options and quality of content at the top of the list of factors to consider.

This report provides an overview of the various types of e-book platforms available to academic, research, public, and K–12 libraries in the United States (and beyond), with a special focus on the products that house electronic versions of books also available in print (thus preserving the original "container" in a digital environment). Platforms covered include e-book–lending services like OverDrive and 3M on the public library side and Brain Hive on the K–12 side; major aggregator platforms like e-books on EBSCOhost and ProQuest's ebrary; research platforms providing reference content only, including Literati by Credo and the Gale Virtual Reference Library; single-publisher–populated e-platforms like SAGE Knowledge and De Gruyter Online; and the platforms housing monographic content by university presses, such as University Press Scholarship Online.

The report does not include journal platforms or the electronic resources known in the library world as databases, unless e-books are their integral component and are available alongside other types of content, such as journals. Good examples of platforms that provide e-books alongside journals include JSTOR and Project MUSE, as well as established STM platforms like SpringerLink and Elsevier's ScienceDirect. The report also does not include e-book platforms available for individual use unless they are also available to libraries. Examples of platforms with consumer as well as institutional pricing options include Cengage Learning's Questia and Scholastic's Storia.

The focus of the report is on the e-book platforms sold to libraries by the vendors with an established presence in the library market, including publishers, aggregators, book distributors, wholesalers, and technology companies. As their products show, they have chosen different strategies to sell e-book content, but their basic goals are similar: to help libraries deliver e-books via business models that meet the needs of library patrons as well as those of the companies that produce the e-books. The aim here is to elucidate the details of each of those business models and to give librarians a summary of the e-book landscape. Librarians may use this report as a starting point in their hunt for e-books or to familiarize themselves with the array of options available to them. The report may also be useful to new-to-the-profession librarians or LIS students needing a crash course on the intricacies of e-book purchasing.

Open-access e-book platforms are excluded from this report, as they warrant a separate discussion and their unique purpose and business model make it difficult to compare them with the platforms sold to libraries via elaborate purchasing plans. These include sites like Unglue.it, DOAB (Directory of Open Access Books), OAPEN (Open Access Publishing in European Networks), and SciELO Books (Scientific Electronic Library Online), to name a few. Likewise, public-domain e-book platforms that provide free access to the content in public domain, such as Internet Archive, Project Gutenberg, HathiTrust, World Public Library, Big Universe, and Children's Books Online, are also excluded as they serve an entirely different purpose. However, libraries with limited e-book budgets will find great value in them and are encouraged to explore all alternatives to for-fee platforms in their efforts to bring e-books to their patrons.

Note: While this report covers the majority of the e-book platforms used in academic, public, and school libraries in the United States, it does not claim to include every e-book platform available to such libraries. A product may have been overlooked for one of two reasons: the author wasn't aware of its existence at the time this report was compiled, or the companies contacted did not inform the author of all available offerings. Since e-book platforms continue to evolve at a rapid pace, librarians are advised to continually monitor the progress of products of interest, as information about their scope and functionalities changes on a quarterly, monthly, and even weekly basis, as well as to keep pace with the new platforms entering the e-book market each year.

Marketplace Basics

Companies that sell e-book content to libraries start out with the same objective—to deliver books digitally to library patrons—but along the way they take different paths to get there. Their varied business models often reflect the corporate structure of each company as well as the technological advances and the changing research needs or reading habits of the users. In the case of e-book lending services like OverDrive or Follett, the end user is usually a public or school library patron looking to check out the latest best seller and download it onto his or her reading device. In the case of research platforms like SAGE Knowledge, it is an undergraduate or graduate student perusing a subject-specific reference source on the library computer.

Technology continues to do its part in transforming the ways in which readers absorb e-book content, both for entertainment and for scholarly inquiry, with one key factor driving the rise in popularity of e-books: the staggering proliferation of hand-held devices in recent years. Because e-book content is now more portable than before and the devices needed to make it portable are more affordable, libraries are in a better position to lend e-books or make their content available for research purposes.

There is no shortage of e-book platforms to choose from, whatever the library's needs. And while the plethora of options may be welcome by some, others see it as an obstacle contributing to confusion and product fatigue for both librarians purchasing platforms and patrons using them to gain access to e-books. Still, there is a flip side to platform fatigue: librarians may gain more value in the long run, and having choices may alleviate some of the anxiety of being stuck in an undesirable situation with only one vendor. Whatever their opinions on this issue, librarians will often find themselves comparing apples and oranges when choosing among e-book platforms, but they will also quickly discover that they can always find what they are looking for if they take the time to get to know the market.

Purchasing of e-books usually starts with the consideration of the source of the content. Librarians may choose to purchase directly from the original curator (i.e., publisher), one of many aggregators (whose platforms offer content from multiple publishers), or distributors (companies that sell e-books from everyone in the information chain, both publishers and aggregators). As library vendors continue to experiment with business models and take advantage of the technologies available to them, it has become more challenging to define the roles of distributors versus aggregators—even wholesalers—as many have dramatically expanded their roles in recent years. Some aggregators, for example, have taken on the roles of both distributors and publishers, while some publishers have opted to distribute their own e-book content in addition to making it widely available via other platforms. In a print environment, it was easier to define the roles of library vendors. In the e-book market, however, the lines have started to blur, making it necessary for librarians to pay close attention to where the content is coming from to avoid both confusion and content overlap.

Publisher E-book Platforms

Libraries acquiring trade titles don't have the option to purchase e-books directly from publishers like Random House, since those books are usually available through e-book lending services, such as, for example,

OverDrive and 3M. On the academic side, quite a few publishers have pursued their own e-book initiatives, releasing platforms that house e-versions of their own titles. Publishers like Oxford University Press, SAGE, and Springer, for example, have made great strides in improving functionalities of their platforms and discoverability of their content. As a result, their products often feature tools just as sophisticated as those by major aggregators.

Since science and technology content ages more rapidly than other types of content—owing to time-sensitive advancements in the STM field—STM publishers faced the e-book challenge long before others and have positioned themselves as leaders on the e-book front. On the K–12 side, the industry has, in recent years, seen the proliferation of platforms featuring interactive e-books, such as those by Scholastic and Rosen Publishing, as well as web-based e-book platforms, such as epointbooks.com, which hosts the titles of several imprints, including Rosen Publishing, Gareth Stevens Publishing, Britannica Educational Publishing, and Windmill Books.

There are many advantages for libraries wanting to buy directly from publishers, including the elimination of middlemen in the process, which saves libraries time and money, and the ability to search across content formats without significant restrictions. (Many publisher platforms fully integrate e-book chapters with journal articles, making it easy for students to peruse e-books and journals on the same topic simultaneously.) Librarians opting for publisher platforms often discover that publishers are more open to negotiations than large aggregators and will work with librarians to accommodate their unique needs.

Publisher platforms also feature a more "organic" look and are equipped with publisher-nurtured enhancements, including maintenance by on-site editors and other staff members familiar with the content. Their platforms may also contain content not available in an aggregator version of their books, particularly multimedia enhancements. On the flip side, working with multiple publishers simultaneously means signing multiple agreements, which requires juggling and business acumen. Plus, there is more to keep up with, as librarians (and patrons) need to get trained each time a new publisher platform is implemented.

Aggregator E-book Platforms

Aggregators include companies that amass e-book content from multiple publishers and sell it to libraries via a range of buying plans. They tend to be more established in academic libraries, since much of their e-book content is intended for use by students, faculty, and scholars. However, many aggregators are releasing public library and K–12 versions of their legacy platforms, and their presence in schools and public libraries is expected to grow. E-books on aggregator platforms are fully searchable and cross-searchable and may be acquired in several ways. Just about every major library aggregator offers its own unique business model. Librarians need to familiarize themselves with the peculiarities of each before deciding what works for their digital environments.

Since aggregators were the early players in the e-book market, their products are often ahead of the curve in terms of technical capabilities and purchasing options. Major aggregator platforms include e-books on EBSCOhost, ProQuest's ebrary, and Ingram's MyiLibrary. Others include EBL (by Ebooks Corporation Limited; acquired by ProQuest in January 2013), Safari Books Online, Books24x7, Knovel, and, for reference e-books, the Gale Virtual Reference Library and Literati by Credo. When buying from aggregators, librarians are dealing with one versus many license agreements, and the ordering is easier since aggregators are fully integrated into distribution systems. Another advantage is that aggregators provide many more titles in one place and are often marketed to libraries as "solution" platforms with a host of embedded discovery services and features that extend beyond providing access to the content, including interactive learning tools and lesson plans.

Since aggregator platforms are publisher-neutral, they are likely to give as much exposure to best-selling titles as to those published by small presses. On the other hand, not all titles from every publisher are available, and many are not available in e-book format as soon as they are published in print (owing to embargo periods set by publishers in advance). Lastly, although they provide access to large quantities of content, aggregator platforms usually come with a high price tag, often impose minimum purchase requirements, and don't allow much room for negotiation since e-book prices, like embargo periods, are mandated by publishers.

Distributors and E-book Lending Services

It has become difficult to set distributors apart from aggregators, as both engage in similar e-book practices and the explosion of new technologies has paved the way for significant expansion of distributor and aggregator roles in the library market. Distributors usually distribute e-books to libraries in an à la carte fashion, include large quantities of popular titles heavily circulated in public libraries, and generally do not make the e-books on their platforms cross-searchable. Distributors' main mission is to circulate e-books on a title-by-title basis rather than to "integrate" them or use them to develop "offspring" collections.

For the purposes of this report, distributors include both wholesalers migrating to the e-model, such as, for example, Baker & Taylor, as well as lending e-book services like OverDrive and Follett, which have dominated e-book distribution in public and school libraries for a number of years. Although wholesalers and e-book lending services may not appear to have much in common, both types of companies generally operate on a one book/one user business model. This means that an item can be checked out for an established period of time by one user. In addition, their titles are coded with DRM (digital rights management) to limit access after the due date.

When e-books started to gain momentum in libraries, print wholesalers were not equipped to handle digital transactions as their systems were based on the traditional print model. But owing to new technologies, they are able to transform their practices and develop digital media platforms of their own. Baker & Taylor's Axis 360 platform makes it possible for libraries to acquire all content in one place. This is especially beneficial for libraries already using Baker & Taylor for their print collections. Purchasing e-books through wholesalers allows for a great deal of flexibility, too. Librarians may purchase single or multiple e-books from many different publishers and aggregators, and they can negotiate their licenses directly with the wholesaler (e.g., Yankee Book Peddler offers e-books from ebrary, EBL, and EBSCOhost). However, e-book prices and licensing terms are set by the publishers, not wholesalers.

University Press Consortium E-book Platforms

When e-books started to gain acceptance across academia, university presses realized that their monograph content needed to be digitized quickly but didn't have the means or the resources to implement new workflows required to digitize their backlists. Instead, they turned to the more established players in the business to make their content available in e-book format. This has given rise to four digitization initiatives supporting the academic market: Oxford University Press's University Press Scholarship Online (UPSO); Cambridge University Press's University Publishing Online (UPO); University Press Content Consortium's (UPCC) Book Collections on Project MUSE; and Books at JSTOR.

Oxford's UPSO and Cambridge's UPO launched in Fall 2011, representing the efforts of two leading university presses using their existing platforms as the foundation to digitize their own backlists as well as those of partner presses. UPSO is a collaboration between Oxford and several other university presses (including Fordham and University of Florida) to aggregate monograph content into a single, cross-searchable platform. UPO is also hosted by a university press with a long history of scholarly publishing, but it casts the net wider. The result of a joint venture between Cambridge University Press and partner publishers (including Liverpool University and Mathematical Association of America), UPO integrates scholarly books with journal articles on a single platform.

The Project MUSE and JSTOR models represent the initiatives of well-known aggregators in the library community that saw an opportunity to build a bridge between librarians and university partners at a time when their means to digitize their own content were limited. While hoping to emulate the successes they've had with journals, both Project MUSE and JSTOR are marrying scholarly books to journals and incorporating other types of content into their growing platforms.

E-book Platforms in Academic and Research Libraries

Academic libraries have for the most part mastered the shift from print to digital on the journal front. E-books are perceived as the next digital frontier. E-book concerns in academic libraries extend beyond circulation issues and involve questions about how e-book platforms support the research needs of students and faculty. Academic vendors are therefore expected to provide the tools and services that help students and faculty deepen and simplify their research at the same time. This has led to the merging of e-book and journal content in a number of platforms.

Whether via advisory boards or through feedback provided to their vendor representatives, academic librarians have had a lot to do with why more e-book platforms now feature journal content as an integral part. In fact, merging e-books and journals is seen as the next big movement in academic library collection development and simply the nature of the beast spawned by technology—one especially welcomed by librarians focusing on information literacy instruction. Many have argued that by not having to explore different vehicles for each kind of information source, instructors can focus on teaching better strategies for using the information itself.

E-book Platforms in Public Libraries

Main e-book controversies in public libraries continue to revolve around e-book lending policies as many trade publishers maintain their imposed restrictions on e-book circulation (e.g., HarperCollins has an imposed limit of 26 checkouts on their e-books, while Random House continues to raise e-book prices, in some cases by 300 percent) and several others (e.g., Hachette) remain uneasy about making their e-books available for library lending. As of early 2013, complications surrounding e-book lending in public libraries showed no signs of slowing down, but progress has been made with some publishers previously hesitant to sell e-books to libraries. In late 2012, Penguin embarked on a new e-book pilot program with the New York and Brooklyn Public Libraries to allow patrons of the two systems to check out Penguin titles six months after publication via 3M Cloud Library, which already partners with Penguin's sister company Random House.

Public libraries have several e-book lending services to choose from, both for adult and K–12 content, with OverDrive usually the first platform most public librarians turn to when deciding on adding e-books to their library's offerings. OverDrive remains the only platform currently offering books on Kindle (owing to OverDrive's partnership with Amazon) and no other platform for public libraries has as many "big publisher" titles. However, OverDrive's domination started to be challenged in late 2011 when 3M entered the e-book market as a direct competitor. 3M is a cloud-based e-book lending system that lets patrons read and check out titles at home, on the go, or via discovery terminals (or kiosks) located inside the library.

A number of public libraries have started experimenting with purchasing books directly from publishers as opposed to committing to a single e-book lending platform. A good example is Douglas County Libraries (CO) model, which has received a lot of attention from the library community and significant interest from publishers. The library hosts its own e-book content on an Adobe Content Server (ACS) and is able to purchase directly from hundreds of publishers at a discount. Patrons are able to borrow thousands of e-books from the collection, while the library claims the ownership of the titles after purchasing them (the way they used to do with print books). This "buy, own, distribute as you'd like" model created by Douglas County Libraries has been picked up by hundreds of libraries across the United States and promises to gain an even larger following in the future.

E-book Platforms in K–12 and School Libraries

Like academic librarians, school and K–12 librarians look for ways to tie digital content to information literacy as more emphasis is placed on educating children at a young age about the types of learning resources available to them. Educators are drawn to "enhanced" e-books that provide embedded tools allowing students to enrich the reading experience by creating storyboards and blogs, writing book reviews and e-mails, and even building wiki pages and websites. Several well-known K–12 publishers have already successfully launched a series of interactive e-books designed to meet the needs of AASL (American Association of School Librarians) standards as well as to support transliteracy skills among K–12 students. These books engage students (at various reading stages) by encouraging them to create their own content within the books. They also engage parents and educators with embedded lesson plans, suggested classroom activities, quizzes, and more.

K–12 librarians expect e-book platforms to include embedded tools that help educators do their job better. They are also on the lookout for platforms fully aligned with the Common Core, a nationwide initiative that calls for a deeper understanding of the context behind each text a student encounters, to be gained via discussions and close readings of primary sources (rather than traditional textbooks). When the Common Core first began to make waves in 2010, reference publishers in particular were quick to recognize the value of their content—especially in digital form—for educators implementing the new standards in their curriculums. This is why we have witnessed more releases (and re-releases) of e-book platforms strongly aligned with (and supporting) Common Core coming from major aggregators such as, for example, EBSCO, as well as publishers like Infobase, which offers a range of subject-specific e-book resources supporting the Common Core.

Major K–12 e-book aggregators include Follett and Mackin. Both platforms are designed to enhance students' research experience via a purchase-to-own acquisition model and both support use of multimedia to enhance learning in K–12 settings, but there are some notable differences. Mackin is a web-based portal that integrates all of its e-books and databases (from well over twenty publishers). The platform supports a number of classroom research activities but does not yet allow for books to be checked out individually. Follett, on the other hand, offers a larger number of selections of e-books, which can be checked out or downloaded for reading either on a web browser or a mobile device.

Chapter 2

Criteria for Purchasing E-book Platforms

Abstract

Chapter 2 of Library Technology Reports *(vol. 49, no. 3) "E-book Platforms for Libraries" covers the criteria librarians usually consider when deciding which platforms to choose as delivery vehicles for their e-book collections. These criteria are divided into four distinct groups: content, technical specifications, functionality, and business model. While the needs of institutions vary greatly even within similar library markets, some key factors have been established within the library community as a way to guide librarians in deciding which platforms best suit their needs. This chapter examines those needs by explaining the importance of the scope of the content (e.g., number of titles included, number of publishers represented, etc.), the product's unique features (e.g., ADA compliance), and the intricate details regarding access to the content and ways in which libraries can purchase it.*

There is no one-size-fits-all model when deciding which platforms to choose for delivery of e-books. Every library's needs are different, and no two products provide the same features and functionalities—even when catering to the same type of library audience. Librarians usually start to get acquainted with a platform (or vendor) by asking questions about the content available and compatibility to make sure that they have the equipment in place to support the product. Then they move on to questions about the terms of the licensing agreement and a host of other topics that usually have to do with one of the following areas: content, technical specifications, functionality, and business model.

Content

Questions pertaining to content can usually be answered by simply browsing each product's website. Publishers and vendors tend to be forthright about the scope of their platforms. It is important to get a good sense of how big these platforms are to understand the logic behind their complex pricing structures. And these platforms run the gamut: from those hosting hundreds of thousands of e-books to those hosting a few hundred titles by one or two publishers. A rule of thumb applies: the greater the scope, the greater the value; the greater the value, the higher the price.

The following content-specific questions usually arise in discussions with library vendors: How many books are included overall? Do I need to purchase all of them? What library markets is the platform built for? Who is the primary audience? What types of e-books are available on the platform (e.g., reference books, trade titles from major houses, monographs)? In the case of subject-specific or publisher-specific e-book platforms, what are the key subjects covered? And how often are new titles added to the platform?

When examining aggregator and distributor platforms, librarians want to know about the overall number of publishers represented to determine how many of those publishers' titles they can expect to circulate in the library. Keeping up with titles and publishers is no small task, since most e-book platforms are updated on a monthly, and some on a weekly, basis. Major aggregators are constantly signing new deals and announcing new partnerships with publishers to boost their offerings.

For research and learning purposes, librarians will want to know about the inclusion of multimedia in the package. Are there videos, images, and other tools that help enhance the reading experience? What about integration of other types of content? What else is included in the package other than e-books? Journals? Databases? Lastly, is there a sister product associated with the platform that librarians should be aware of?

Here is an outline of the various content factors to consider when choosing e-book platforms:

- type of e-book platform (e.g., by publisher, aggregator, wholesaler, university press, e-book lending service)
- primary library market (e.g., public, K–12, academic, corporate, government)
- number of titles
- number of publishers and/or imprints
- types of e-books on the platform (e.g., trade books, reference books, monographs, K–12 nonfiction)
- expected growth/frequency of updates (how often new titles are added)
- subjects covered (e.g., fiction, general nonfiction, arts and humanities, science and technology)
- inclusion of multimedia (e.g., images, videos, interactive maps)
- integration of content other than e-books (e.g., journals)
- inclusion of book reviews
- inclusion of author biographies and other works by the same author
- distributor partner (e.g., Yankee Book Peddler)
- offspring (related products)

Technical Specifications

Technical specs involve discussions about the equipment needed for the library or user to access e-books, browsers supported, software or plugins needed, file formats of e-books, and compatible e-readers. Most e-book platforms support all browsers, including Internet Explorer, Safari, and Firefox, but some are still not compatible with Google Chrome, for example. Librarians need to keep in mind that not all patrons own portable reading devices and may still be reading e-books on their home computers. Knowing in advance which browsers the platform supports and whether any additional software installations are needed (e.g., Adobe Digital Editions) will determine if the e-book platform reflects the needs of their community.

E-books are generally sold to libraries in PDF and ePub file formats. These two formats are supported by the majority of reading devices, including Nook, iPad, Sony eReader, and Kobo. Kindle uses its own proprietary format known as AZW. ePub is considered to be the industry standard preferred by librarians. Most vendors whose platforms support only PDF are working toward making their e-books available in ePub. Librarians usually recommend buying e-books in ePub, XHTML, or other XML-based formats because the files are reflowable and can better adapt their presentation to the output device. PDF files generally do not adapt as well to mobile devices and are difficult to view on small screens. If PDF is the only file format offered by the vendor, text-based Adobe PDF formats are a good alternative as they support highlighting, keyword searching, and disability access.

Clearly, not all e-books may be read on all devices. This is one of the most challenging aspects of how e-books have evolved in recent years. While the number of dedicated e-readers continues to grow, so does the frustration surrounding the limitations imposed on users who own only one reading device or a library able to afford only one type of e-book platform. The most prevalent portable e-readers include Barnes & Noble's Nook, Apple's iPad, Sony's eReader, Kobo, and Amazon's Kindle. The Kindle is widely considered to be the most user-friendly e-book reading device since it uses the patron's Amazon account as the delivery source for content.

Here is an outline of the technical factors to consider when choosing e-book platforms:

- browsers supported (e.g., Internet Explorer, Safari, Firefox, Google Chrome)
- software requirements (e.g., Adobe Digital Editions)
- plugin requirements
- file formats (e.g., ePub, PDF, HTML)
- availability of an app
- hand-held e-readers supported (e.g., Nook, iPad, Kindle, Kobo, Sony eReader)
- availability of a proprietary reader by the vendor
- compatibility with ILS (integrated library system)
- integration with the library's OPAC

Functionality

Functionality is all about the bells and whistles associated with each platform. Librarians need to be aware of the different features available and how valuable they may be both to the library (e.g., COUNTER reports) and to the patrons (e.g., ability to print). Academic librarians will be most interested in the embedded tools that support research, including full-text searching at book and chapter level, annotation and citation tools, persistent URLs, generous copy/paste and printing options, and content availability for offline reading.

The availability of usage data (e.g., COUNTER), ADA-compliant features, and MARC records are of interest to all libraries. E-book catalogs can range from having MARC records available for every e-book title offered by the library to not having any. The majority of vendors, especially those with a large number of reference books, provide MARC records.

Here is an outline of the various functionality factors to consider when choosing e-book platforms:

- full-text searching
- keyword searching
- copy/paste options
- printing options
- downloading options
- searching at article, book, and collection level
- advanced search capabilities (truncation, Boolean)
- bookmarking within e-books
- citation tools
- annotation tools
- offline reading
- availability of usage reports
- persistent URLs (book, chapter, collection level)
- print-on-demand copy service
- ADA compliance
- personalization features
- availability of MARC records

Business Models

Dealing with business models and understanding the multitude of pricing options available is the most complicated—and controversial—part of e-book acquisition. It requires constantly keeping up with various policies and business practices, which change continually owing to the mergers that occur within the industry and to the technological advances that make it possible for companies to upgrade purchasing plans more frequently. Many questions need to be answered before a library can sign a contract with a vendor and commit to an e-book platform. Since pricing options are usually not explained at length on vendor sites, librarians need to take a proactive approach and explore all viable alternatives.

Here is a sampling of typical business model questions a vendor sales representative may encounter: Is this a subscription platform or purchase-to-own business model? If I choose to purchase e-books to own, are there annual access fees associated with using the platform? Can they be waived if a certain number of e-books are purchased in advance? If I opt for a subscription package, what happens to the content after my contract expires? How frequently will my library be invoiced? Can I view the product before purchasing (and without needing to sign up for an institutional trial)? What DRM policies should I be aware of? And what about embargoes? How long will my library need to wait before it can offer best-selling titles? Although publishers don't wait as long as they used to to release e-versions of print titles, some still impose an embargo period before e-book versions are available for library lending.

Since many e-book vendors charge the cost of a print title plus a certain percentage for their e-books, librarians want to know what the cost of each title is in relation to its print counterpart. They also want to know about single versus multiple versus unlimited use of each e-book. Some platforms allow for an unlimited use of their e-books (by any number of readers at any time), while others adhere to a one title/one user model. Some offer unlimited access for older titles but impose a one title/one user model for new releases. Access policies vary widely among vendors, and they are not always set in stone. If a vendor has only one business model in place at launch, it is not unusual for the vendor to revise its policy in six months to offer more options.

Patron-driven acquisition (PDA) is one of the most talked-about models for acquiring e-books in academic libraries. Offered by both publishers and aggregators, the PDA model is fairly straightforward: e-book purchases are triggered based on traffic and patron interest in particular titles. In other words, patrons' use of a book triggers purchase. (Various trigger and price points are offered.) This business model guarantees that only the content that gets used gets purchased. Although it is not as common in public libraries, some vendors, including 3M, have started experimenting with a PDA option for their public library customers.

Short-term loans (STL) may be a good solution for librarians looking to obtain access to content they wouldn't be able to afford buying. STLs are similar to the PDA model in that patron demand ultimately drives what the library budget is spent on. The key difference is that STLs are about renting e-books instead of buying them. Patrons borrow titles directly from the aggregator's catalog (not owned by the library) and get access to a title for a set period of time (usually one, two, three, seven, fourteen, or thirty days) and the library is charged for the rental. This costs the library anywhere from 5 to 30 percent of the title price. (Loan prices escalate according to the number of days required for the loan.)

One popular way to save money when purchasing e-books is via library consortia. Many vendors have arrangements with consortia that provide e-books to libraries at discounted rates. As is the case with other alternatives, librarians will encounter both benefits and drawbacks when choosing the consortial route. Benefits include more e-books for less money and equality of content across libraries; minimal energy spent on licensing agreements; and e-book lending across a wide variety of libraries. There are also challenges to note. Since publishers don't benefit as much when libraries share access, they often put pressure on aggregators to limit the size of consortia. In addition, certain member libraries may have unique needs that are not in line with those of other members, or they may not want to spend money on titles that others want to buy. On the public library side, larger consortia mean longer queues of popular trade titles.

Here is an outline of the business model factors to consider when choosing e-book platforms:

- one user/one book model
- purchase-to-own option
- subscription option
- short-term loans
- patron-driven acquisition (PDA)
- free viewing period (for PDA)
- perpetual archive fee
- title cost relative to print cost
- minimum commitment
- interlibrary loan (ILL)
- invoicing intervals (monthly, quarterly, yearly)
- DRM policies
- use of content via classroom projection devices (e.g., interactive whiteboards)
- annual maintenance fee
- free trials (length)
- pay-per-view option
- availability of prebuilt subject collections
- consortial purchasing
- approval plans
- embargo period

Chapter 3

Directory of E-book Platforms for Libraries

Abstract

Chapter 3 of Library Technology Reports *(vol. 49, no. 3) "E-book Platforms for Libraries," the main part of the report, is an A–Z directory of fifty-one e-book platforms competing for the attention of purchasing librarians in the United States and around the world. Each platform is placed in the context of its respective library market and identified according to platform type (e.g., aggregator, publisher), library market (e.g., academic/research, public), e-book type (e.g., trade books, reference books, etc.), and subjects covered (e.g., general, science, humanities, etc.). Special attention is given to unique features of each product.*

The following is an A–Z listing of major e-book platforms available to libraries looking to purchase academic, professional, trade, and K–12 e-books. Each platform is described and identified according to the following characteristics:

- **Library markets:** academic/research, corporate, government, public, K–12, etc.
- **Platform type:** aggregator, distributor, e-book lending service, publisher, university press consortium (If a platform serves a dual purpose, it is identified accordingly, e.g., aggregator/distributor.)
- **E-book type:** handbooks, reference books, trade nonfiction, fiction, children's books, etc.
- **Main subjects:** general, science, humanities, arts, social sciences, etc.
- **Background:** a concise description of the platform, its unique features, and the company's vision for the product
- **Business model:** a brief explanation of purchasing options and plans available to libraries

123Library

Website: https://www.123library.org
Parent company: 123Doc Education
Library markets: academic/research
Platform type: aggregator/distributor
E-book type: scholarly publications, textbooks, general nonfiction
Main subjects: science, technology, health, medicine, social science, humanities

Background: The United Kingdom's largest distributor of academic e-books, 123Library is marketed to libraries as a universal platform that works with all computer systems and mobile devices. Its web-based e-book reader (123FastReader) preserves the original formatting of each page as published in print—beneficial for libraries acquiring illustrated books. The company partners with a wide range of publishers to distribute academic, textbook, and trade content to libraries, including Hodder Education, SAGE Publications, Informa Healthcare, Elsevier, and Wiley-Blackwell. It has a strong presence in the European e-book market. Over 100 new e-books in the field of health care are added each month. Basic search is a Google-style single input field that recognizes ISBNs as distinct from other values. Advanced search allows users to restrict search to books or journals (or both).

Business Model: Librarians may browse the online catalog and purchase one book at a time or opt for a range of prepackaged collections of e-books. Several business models are supported, including outright purchase of e-books (once you buy e-books, you own them outright) and the loan/pay-per-view/PDA option, which allows institutions to have large collections of e-books available for a small access fee; pay only for e-books that have been read; purchase e-books gradually (10 percent at a time); or acquire titles in perpetuity.

3M Cloud Library

Website: http://ebook.3m.com
Parent company: 3M
Library markets: public
Platform type: distributor/e-book lending service
E-book type: trade fiction and nonfiction
Main subjects: all

Background: 3M's cloud-based e-book lending service launched in the summer of 2011 and gained in popularity throughout 2012. It comprises over 250,000 e-book titles for adults from over 300 publishers, including HarperCollins, Random House, Penguin, ABC-CLIO, Baker Publishing Group, John Wiley & Sons, and Workman Publishing. Patrons can read and check out titles at home or on the go. They can also use Discovery Terminal Downloads stations in the library, which let them browse the catalog. To check out books, they can use 3M's own e-reader hardware, which synchronizes with 3M Cloud Library. It doesn't require a credit card and patrons do not need to buy it. The system is compatible with PCs, Macs, iPads, and Nooks.

Business Model: 3M Cloud Library operates on a one user/one e-book model. Libraries retain use of purchased content even after they leave the service, and they can transfer content to another platform once their contract expires. 3M also offers a PDA option called the "Wish List." It allows patrons to place titles on a wish list. If their library decides to purchase a book on this list, it is automatically delivered to the patron.

ABC-CLIO eBook Collection

Website: http://ebooks.abc-clio.com
Parent company: ABC-CLIO
Library markets: academic/research, public, K–12
Platform type: publisher
E-book type: encyclopedias, dictionaries, handbooks
Main subjects: history, social sciences, humanities, LIS (library and information science)

Background: ABC-CLIO's is a research platform with over 7,000 e-books, ranging from encyclopedias and dictionaries to handbooks and guides published by ABC-CLIO as well as its other imprints: Greenwood, Libraries Unlimited, Praeger, and Linworth. The e-books are cross-searchable and include citations in four formats, e-mail and print capabilities, personalized bookmarks and notes, free downloadable MARC records, and remote accessibility of content. On the product's website, librarians may download (in Excel) the entire list of titles in the collection, broken down by major subject areas, imprint, pub date, and ISBN. Subject collections include world history, popular culture, literature, military history, security studies, and women's studies, among others. Other features include direct deep linking and mobile device capability via web browser.

Business Model: ABC-CLIO allows for unlimited, simultaneous user access to its e-book platform, which fully supports commuting and off-campus students and online courses. Educators are encouraged to use the platform in classroom settings.

Axis 360

Website: http://btol.com/axis360
Parent company: Baker & Taylor
Library markets: public, K–12, government, corporate, academic
Platform type: distributor/wholesaler
E-book type: popular trade fiction and nonfiction, best sellers, reference books, scholarly publications
Main subjects: all

Background: Baker & Taylor's e-book platform, Axis 360 (live since late 2011), makes it possible for libraries to acquire library content—including books, e-books, audiobooks, videos, and music—in one place. The content can be read on Blio—ADA-compliant multimedia e-reading software that specializes in preserving the look of physical items in digital environments—as well as Barnes & Noble's Nook, Sony's eReader, and Kobo. Librarians can choose from about 400,000 e-books (in ePub, PDF, or .xps format) through Baker & Taylor's Title Source 3 at the same time they order print titles. The platform surfaces content on a "magic wall," allowing patrons to check out the e-books they want, browse by subject, get recommendations for additional reading, and contribute book reviews. The platform is fully compatible with assistive screen-reader technologies, including JAWS, Window-Eyes, NVDA (nonvisual desktop access), and System Access to Go. Benefits for librarians include embedded collection development services, full ILS integration, immediate activation of ordered titles, and a library-branded platform.

Business Model: Purchase of any e-book enables a library to circulate the content in all available formats without needing to buy individual file types. Single-user and multiuser access models from participating publishers are available as of 2013 (but were not available at launch). Baker & Taylor is exploring other business models, including short-term loans, demand-driven acquisition, and classroom adoptions. It also provides libraries the option to offer content purchasing from its Axis 360 service via a Buy Now option, which links to e-commerce transactions that ship directly to patrons' homes and generate revenue for the institution.

Books24x7

Website: www.books24x7.com
Parent company: Skillsoft Ireland Limited
Library markets: academic/research, corporate
Platform type: aggregator/distributor
E-book type: reference books, handbooks, monographs, reports
Main subjects: computer science, engineering, business, government, public administration

Background: A subsidiary of Skillsoft since 2001, Books24x7 was one of the earliest companies to license and repackage e-books for IT professionals on a subscription basis. It provides online access to the unabridged contents of books; book summaries; and leadership, IT, and desktop videos via fifteen topical collections, among them ITPro, Leadership Development Channel videos (in English or in languages with subtitles and localized metadata), fifty Lessons videos, Skillsoft IT and Desktop Videos, BusinessPro, EngineeringPro, FinancePro, OfficeEssentials, Well-BeingEssentials, ExecSummaries, ExecBlueprints, and GovEssentials. These collections include the full text of thousands of professional books; live and on-demand videos of business leaders; best practices from executives of Fortune 5000 companies; and full reports from and summaries of the analyst community. New titles are added every week, and the product is expected to increase to 39,000 titles by the end of 2013. Key features include complimentary MARC records, a patented search interface, and productivity tools that include bookmarks, notes, personal folders, multiple citation formats, RefWorks, and persistent URLs.

Business Model: Books24x7's goal is to monetize publishers' content through sales of whole books as well as licensing fees. It has a Buy Book link on every page in its offerings. Although the default bookseller is Amazon, publishers can redirect the link to any online bookseller. Libraries can subscribe to any combination of the topical collections. Books24x7 offers site licenses and concurrent seat licensing models based on FTE (full-time equivalent).

Books at JSTOR

Website: http://books.jstor.org
Parent company: ITHAKA
Library markets: academic/research
Platform type: university press consortium
E-book type: monographs, scholarly publications
Main subjects: humanities, sciences, arts, social sciences

Background: Books at JSTOR is an initiative by several university presses (including Yale, Princeton, Columbia, and Cornell, among others) to make their e-books available as part of JSTOR, a research platform founded in 1995 by the Andrew W. Mellon Foundation. The 15,000 e-books are cross-searchable with millions of journal articles and primary sources already on JSTOR. (Patrons may select tabs at the top of the Search Results page in order to limit results by content type.) A wide range of scholarly disciplines is represented, including, for example, technology, history, music, political science, education, sociology, business, and law. The platform also includes a million book reviews. Books are preserved in Portico, ITHAKA's digital preservation service.

Business Model: E-books are available for purchase under a single-user or an unlimited-user model. The single-user model is offered for all books and allows for thirty downloads per year, with ability to purchase more. The unlimited concurrent user model includes unlimited, DRM-free downloads and can be upgraded to the single-user model. A demand-driven acquisition (DDA) model is available for some (not all) titles, and purchases are triggered when certain usage thresholds are met. Pricing is tiered according to JSTOR classifications; volume discounts are available.

Books@Ovid

Website: http://site.ovid.com/site/products/books_landing.jsp
Parent company: Ovid Technologies, Inc. (Wolters Kluwer)
Library markets: academic/research
Platform type: aggregator/distributor
E-book type: textbooks, reference books, manuals, handbooks
Main subjects: health, medicine, nursing, psychiatry

Background: Books@Ovid provides full-text coverage from a number of medical textbooks and reference books for students and researchers in the health care professions. Most of the titles are published by Lippincott Williams & Wilkins, a leading medical publisher. Others include Wiley-Blackwell, Springer, and CABI Publishing. A wide range of medical subjects are covered, with special emphasis on clinical practice, including nursing and psychiatry. Users can browse the collection by title or subject, and they may choose to print individual chapters or sections within the books. Books@Ovid is integrated with Journals@Ovid and Ovid's Bibliographic Databases and includes the following features: multifile searching, links from book bibliographies, book topic links, and results ranked by relevance (not by book title).

Business Model: Libraries may purchase books on an individual basis or select any of the available subject collections. Collection prices depend on the number of titles included in each collection, ranging from ten to fifty.

Brain Hive

Website: www.brainhive.com
Parent company: Brain Hive, LLC
Library markets: K–12
Platform type: distributor/e-book lending service
E-book type: picture books, chapter books, graphic novels, YA fiction and nonfiction
Main subjects: all

Background: Brain Hive is a pay-as-you-go, on-demand e-book service for K–12 schools that launched in 2012. Available on the platform are some 3,500 titles from twenty publishers, among them Random House, Lerner Publishing Group, Gecko Press, the Creative Company, Kane Press, Red Chair Press, and Stoke Books. Dozens of new titles from more publishers are expected to be added each month. The e-books are aligned with STM and Common Core State Standards, and teachers are encouraged to form book clubs and incorporate lessons within the platform's environment. Key features include printable activities, teaching resources, and Accelerated Reader quizzes from Renaissance Learning. E-books can be searched by grade level and subject. A free Brain Hive eReader App for iPad is available through the Apple App Store.

Business Model: Schools have the option to buy the most popular titles on a multiuser basis, which allows them to make the e-books they purchase a permanent part of a library collection. They pay $1 each time an e-book is checked out, with schools having the option to set the loan period at three, seven, or fourteen days. Membership is free, and there are no additional rental fees.

Cambridge Books Online (CBO)

Website: http://ebooks.cambridge.org
Parent company: Cambridge University Press
Library markets: academic/research
Platform type: publisher
E-book type: monographs, textbooks
Main subjects: science, technology, medicine, humanities, social sciences

Background: Newly redesigned for 2013, Cambridge Books Online is a multidisciplinary e-book platform that provides access to about 20,000 titles published by Cambridge University Press. Included are backlist as well as frontlist titles that are made available on the platform within four to six weeks of the print publication date. Key features include compliance with all major industry standards and initiatives and extensive user functionality, including hyperlinked references and personalization options. MARC records are available free of charge for all titles in the collections. Librarians may download a MARC21 format file containing records of all titles to which their institution has purchased access.

Business Model: Libraries can purchase predefined subject collections or come up with packages with their own selection of e-books in a number of purchasing plans, including a perpetual-access model, approval plans, advance ordering, or subscription.

dawsonera

Website: http://dawsonera.com
Parent company: Dawson Books, Ltd.
Library markets: academic/research, professional
Platform type: distributor
E-book type: scholarly publications, monographs, reference books
Main subjects: all

Background: dawsonera is a web-based portal for academic libraries with a strong presence in the European library market. The software is held on the Dawson server. (The library does not install it locally.) It is accessed via the Internet like any other site. The software enables a library to manage a collection of e-books and lend the e-books to their patrons. The Reader Portal is where e-books may be discovered and read (in PDF), while the Admin Portal serves as a tool for librarians to purchase e-books and manage their collections. Publishers that partner with Dawson can obtain information about their e-books via the Publisher Portal. The following academic publishers have an agreement with dawsonera: Blackwell, Brill, Cambridge University Press, Emerald, McGraw-Hill, Oxford University Press, Psychology Press, Routledge, SAGE Publications, Taylor & Francis, Wiley, and a few others.

Business Model: Each library builds a tailored collection of e-books for its patrons, title by title. Once an e-book is purchased, perpetual access is offered to each copy. Alternatively, libraries may choose to temporarily rent e-books not yet purchased. Short-term downloading of e-books from the collection is also possible. Each e-book purchased is charged at the list price set by the publisher, plus a hosting fee. No other charges apply.

De Gruyter Online

Website: www.degruyter.com
Parent company: De Gruyter
Library markets: academic/research
Platform type: publisher
E-book type: scholarly publications, monographs, reference books, textbooks
Main subjects: arts, humanities, social sciences, science, technology, medicine, LIS (library and information science)

Background: De Gruyter Online is a multiproduct platform that houses all of De Gruyter's e-content, including journals, monographs, reference books, and directories in a wide range of subject categories, including history, law, literary studies, medicine, philosophy, theology, and linguistics and communications, among others. The convergence of print and online formats under one roof replaced De Gruyter's previous platform, Reference Global, in early 2012. At the time of its launch, the new platform comprised about 60,000 titles, well over 200,000 book chapters, and nearly 250,000 journal articles. Advanced personalization features allow users to engage with content via content alerts, annotations, saved searches, and personal virtual bookshelves for titles, chapters, and articles. Librarians may subscribe to subject newsletters with eTOC, saved search, and citations alerts. All e-books are full-text searchable, indexed, and enhanced with DOIs and MARC records.

Business Model: E-books can be ordered individually, as pick-and-choose packages, or as fixed packages. Options include perpetual access as well as twenty-four-hour access to individual e-book chapters via pay-per-view. Librarians can buy fixed e-book packages at special rates: subject packages are offered with a 15 percent discount, the complete package with a 20 percent discount on the list prices of the individual titles. As an alternative to fixed packages, libraries can purchase between twenty and fifty e-books for a 5 percent discount or fifty-one or more e-books for a 10 percent discount.

EBL (Ebook Library)

Website: www.eblib.com
Parent company: ProQuest, LLC
Library markets: academic/research, corporate, government
Platform type: aggregator/e-book lending service
E-book type: scholarly publications, reference books, monographs
Main subjects: all

Background: EBL provides e-books to academic, research, government, and corporate libraries, featuring over 350,000 titles from hundreds of publishers representing and covering a range of scholarly disciplines. The e-books can be borrowed and checked out like print books and accessed either online, through EBL's PDF-based reader, or offline (by downloading Adobe Reader to a computer or e-book reading device). Patrons can browse all books and utilize full-text search within the browser. Chapters can be utilized for purchase by students, for reserve lending by libraries, and for inclusion in e-Pack course packs. Stand-out features include an in-browser dictionary, the ability to create and export notes (via RefWorks or e-mail), and a read-aloud tool. Free MARC records with an option for automatic delivery are available for all titles, and other services, such as integrated authentication, automated holdings with OCLC, electronic invoicing and ordering, and real-time budget-tracking tools are available to support the library workflow.

Business Model: EBL offers e-books via several models, including traditional firm order accounts, demand-driven acquisition programs, short-term loans, or any combination of these. Non-Linear Lending, EBL's signature lending system, enables libraries to buy one copy of an e-book (for the price of one book) and lend it simultaneously to multiple patrons. This model limits the total number of lending days per year per title but enables multiple concurrent access. All EBL titles can be downloaded for offline or mobile use and are all eligible for DDA programs.

eBooks on EBSCOhost

Website: http://ebscohost.com/ebooks
Parent company: EBSCO Publishing
Library markets: academic/research, public, K–12, corporate
Platform type: aggregator
E-book type: reference books, scholarly publications, general nonfiction
Main subjects: all

Background: eBooks on EBSCOhost is EBSCO's collection of more than 350,000 (mostly nonfiction and reference) e-books from 1,400 publishers in a wide variety of disciplines and subjects, fully integrated into the EBSCOhost interface. Users may browse high-interest titles in various topic areas and employ the EBSCOhost Collection Manager to select and acquire them. eBook Academic Subscription Collection provides access to thousands of full-text academic e-books. Academic librarians may also opt to own (in perpetuity) EBSCO's Featured Collections, which offer titles covering a range of different topic areas from within a subject. Prepackaged Subject Sets (also owned in perpetuity) focus on a single topic from within a broader subject and contain frontlist titles selected by EBSCO's Collection Development team. eBook Public Library Subscription Collection includes 23,000 titles chosen specifically for public libraries, featuring best-selling and highly recommended titles from leading publishers. EBSCO recently launched its first e-book subscription collection for corporations, aimed at business professionals, with more than 5,600 e-books on leadership and management, finance and accounting, sales, and related topics. MARC records are available at no charge for every title on the platform.

Business Model: eBooks on EBSCOhost are available for purchase via three access models: one user at a time, three simultaneous users, or unlimited users. Subscriptions are available annually to high-interest subject anthologies of e-book titles, while short-term leases are available for one, seven, fourteen, or twenty-eight days. EBSCO also offers a patron-driven acquisition (PDA) program that allows librarians to preselect titles by publisher, subject, or other criteria and then expose them through the library's OPAC; a purchase is triggered only when a book is used. The cost of the books is the individual publisher's list price; there are no additional fees for purchasing libraries. Discounts are available for consortium members.

ebrary

Website: www.ebrary.com
Parent company: ProQuest
Library markets: academic/research, public, K–12, corporate
Platform type: aggregator
E-book type: scholarly publications, general nonfiction
Main subjects: all

Background: Acquired by ProQuest in January 2011, ebrary is a pioneer in the e-book business, with a platform featuring about 450,000 e-book titles from over 500 publishers, including the majority of university presses, leading academic and STM publishers, and a number of trade publishers. Its legacy product is Academic Complete, which features around sixteen subject collections, and Public Complete, which features public library–oriented collections, among them schools and studying, career development, practical life skills, and arts and leisure. In 2012, ebrary announced a three-step approach to e-book acquisition for libraries: transition, diversify, and streamline, with a goal to encourage libraries to transition a greater percentage of their budgets to application programming interfaces (APIs) from print to electronic, diversify acquisition models, and streamline order processes. Full e-books and individual chapters can be downloaded onto various devices, including Kobo and Nook. Additionally, libraries are able to upload and integrate their own content with DASH! (Data Sharing, Fast).

Business Model: Acquisition models include subscription (based on FTE), PDA, short-term loans, and outright purchase through perpetual archive. The short-term loan policy allows users to borrow an e-book from ebrary's catalog for a term, set by the library, of either one day or one week. Each loan costs a library 10 to 30 percent of the e-book price, depending on the length of the loan and ebrary's agreement with the publisher. Libraries are able to offer patrons up to three short-term loans per title, after which they are required to purchase the title for continued access.

epointbooks.com

Website: www.epointbooks.com
Parent company: Rosen Publishing
Library markets: K–12, public
Platform type: publisher
E-book type: children's nonfiction
Main subjects: social studies, history, science, health, math, arts and crafts

Background: epointbooks.com is an e-book platform (powered by MyiLibrary) that provides access to over 3,500 nonfiction titles for the Pre K–12 market from Rosen Publishing, Gareth Stevens Publishing, Britannica Educational Publishing, and Windmill Books. The platform allows users to search content across all purchased titles and bookmark and highlight selected passages. Selected content can be printed or downloaded for offline use, and personal notes and bookmarks can be stored in "subaccounts." With the subaccounts, users can save notes and bookmarks in any e-book, along with previous search results. E-books can be accessed via a library website or a library's catalog using MARC records. Titles are organized by subject and/or publisher-specific collections. Students can load an e-book via any web browser and activate host-based features.

Business Model: E-books are ordered directly from Rosen Publishing like print titles and then loaded into a library's account. The library receives a confirmation e-mail once an e-book order is processed and the selected e-books are loaded into the epointbooks.com account. Discounts for school and public libraries are provided.

Follett eBooks

Website: http://aboutfollettebooks.com
Parent company: Follett Corporation
Library markets: K–12, public
Platform type: distributor/e-book lending service

E-book type: children's and YA fiction and nonfiction, reference books
Main subjects: all

Background: FollettShelf is a free service from Follett Corporation, a distributor of content to public and K–12 libraries, that provides web-based access to all of the company's e-content, including Follett eBooks. Other components of FollettShelf include Capstone Interactive Library, Lerner Interactive Books, Catalist Digital, TumbleBook Library, and Rourke Interactive eBooks. All databases purchased through Follett (e.g., Rosen's Teen & Health Wellness) are also accessed through FollettShelf. Follett e-books are digital editions of print titles with advanced capabilities, many designed for educational purposes. E-books can be previewed and purchased using Follett's Titlewave interface. Some are sold as curriculum-focused and subject-focused bundles designed for use in elementary, middle, and high schools. E-books can be read on a web browser or mobile device, they can be read in the cloud or downloaded for reading, and all have searchable text and a built-in dictionary. In addition, bookmarking can be done manually by students, books can be returned early, and students can highlight text. The Follett Digital Reader app must be installed to read Follett e-books offline. The platform is compatible with Destiny Library Manager ILS.

Business Model: E-books purchased are owned, and there are no access fees. Some are available as single check-outs only, while others allow multiple checkouts of a single copy (about 30,000 of over 145,000 titles). If the e-book is an unlimited simultaneous access Follett e-book, then multiple users can access the title concurrently. If a title is a one-to-one e-book, access is possible for as many users as there are purchased and available copies.

Freading Ebook Service

Website: http://freading.com
Parent company: Library Ideas LLC
Library markets: public
Platform type: distributor/e-book lending service
E-book type: trade fiction and nonfiction, YA fiction and nonfiction
Main subjects: all

Background: Library Ideas is known for its signature music product, Freegal. Freading, a pay-per-use e-book platform for libraries, is its book counterpart. Freading's list of publishers isn't as exhaustive as that of OverDrive and does not include titles from major trade publishers, but a number of well-known mid-size publishers are represented, including Sterling, Sourcebooks, Workman, Algonquin Books, and Kensington. The number of e-books on the platform stands at around 50,000, and new content is added on a weekly basis. Patrons of participating libraries download content through the Freading site via prepaid "tokens," and libraries choose the number of tokens available weekly to them. Freading is not integrated with the library's OPAC and does not supply MARC records, although this service is planned for the near future. Freading's multiuser, simultaneous lending model is attractive to libraries looking to obtain access to ready-made collections and avoid wait lines for lending.

Business Model: The Freading model allows multiple users to read the same title at the same time. After a $150 start-up fee, libraries pay for content as it is selected and used by patrons. Prices range from $.50 to $2 per use, depending on the copyright date of the book. The subscribing library purchases a set number of tokens, and users get a weekly allotment to spend on downloads. Content is never owned, and the loan period is two weeks. Each book can then be renewed for a two-week period for free or for a nominal fee. After the four-week loan period, the book cannot be accessed without incurring a new download fee.

FreedomFlix

Website: http://freedomflix.digital.scholastic.com/home
Parent company: Scholastic, Inc.
Library markets: K–12, public
Platform type: publisher
E-book type: children's nonfiction
Main subjects: social studies, US history

Background: FreedomFlix features Common Core–aligned content from Children's Press's Cornerstones of Freedom book series. All e-books provide an interactive learning experience and are supported with primary sources, videos, audio, images, and related articles. Included are texts and facsimiles of historical documents, videos that build on the living history theme, related articles from Grolier Online, dramatic readings of letters and firsthand accounts, and project ideas. There are also several teacher tools in the package, including a Show What You Know quiz (ten multiple-choice questions); one to three open-ended classroom discussion questions; a lesson plan; and an interactive whiteboard activity. With the Digital Locker preference, students can save and take notes on any page, save where they leave off in the book with the bookmark feature, and highlight and save key assets from the book.

Business Model: Access to the platform may be purchased through Scholastic Library Publishing only. Annual subscriptions for school and public libraries include unlimited, 24/7 multiuser simultaneous and remote access from home. Annual platform fees apply for subscriptions. There is no purchase-to-own option.

Gale Virtual Reference Library (GVRL)

Website: www.gale.cengage.com/gvrl
Parent company: Cengage Learning
Library markets: academic/research, public, K–12
Platform type: aggregator
E-book type: reference books and series nonfiction
Main subjects: all

Background: GVRL, which underwent a significant revision in 2011, is a research e-book platform with approximately 8,000 titles for purchase from more than eighty publishers, including SAGE, Dorling Kindersley, Facts On File, ABC-CLIO, Elsevier, Wiley, and Encyclopædia Britannica. It allows librarians to build digital reference collections title by title, and all purchased e-books are cross-searchable with other Gale content, including InfoTrac and certain In Context products, using Gale PowerSearch. Users can search the entire digital collection, a specific book series, or a chosen title, and bibliographic data can be exported to third-party citation tools. Other features include a user interface in thirty-four languages; ReadSpeaker (text-to-speech functionality) for nineteen languages; on-demand machine-aided content translations into fourteen languages; hundred of titles in Spanish, Chinese, French, and other languages; and an interactive book-like experience with a two-page viewer and page flipper.

Business Model: GVRL is a purchase model. Libraries buy the titles they want and get unlimited simultaneous-user access to them. The purchased e-books are owned indefinitely. There is a nominal hosting fee, used to support the enhancing of the platform.

Infobase eBooks

Website: http://infobaselearning.com/ebooks
Parent company: Infobase Publishing
Library markets: K–12, public, academic
Platform type: publisher
E-book type: reference books, general nonfiction
Main subjects: history, science, literature, health, medicine, careers, biographies, religion, arts

Background: Infobase eBooks contain proprietary content from the following imprints: Facts On File, Chelsea House, Ferguson Publishing, and Bloom's Literary Criticism. It comprises about 4,000 core-curriculum, sole-source titles for middle school through academic-level library patrons, as well as a variety of embedded e-book collections. Features for libraries include unlimited simultaneous use with 24/7 remote access; correlations to Common Core, state, and national standards; no access, hosting, or service fees; citations in MLA, Chicago, and APA formats; free downloadable MARC records; enhanced admin tools; and usage statistics. The platform is organized into twenty-five subject collections for subject-oriented searching. HTML is the default display format (although PDFs are still available, and account administrators can download PDFs to archive).

Business Model: Individual e-books can be purchased in perpetuity, with unlimited simultaneous use and 24/7 access. Libraries may opt for subject-specific e-book collections, which contain the full texts of editorially chosen core-curriculum titles. Master e-book subscriptions are also available for the academic, middle/high school, and public library markets. Individual K–12 schools pay print list price for each e-book. Pricing for multiple schools and academic institutions is based on FTE. Pricing for public libraries is based on the number of card holders.

Knovel

Website: http://why.knovel.com
Parent company: Knovel Corporation
Library markets: academic/research, professional, government
Platform type: aggregator
E-book type: scholarly and professional literature
Main subjects: engineering

Background: Knovel is a collection of over 16,000 full-text (PDF) e-books in science, technology, and engineering that are integrated with Knovel's productivity and data analysis tools that help users manipulate available information. There are nearly 100,000 interactive tables, graphs, and equations in the package. Subscribers also get access to more than 4,000 reference works and databases from more than ninety international publishers and professional societies via the same interface. Subject areas covered are broken down into a number of broad categories, including Adhesives, Sealants, Coatings & Inks; Aerospace & Radar Technology; Biochemistry, Biology & Biotechnology; Ceramics & Ceramic Engineering; Civil Engineering & Construction Materials; Environment & Environmental Engineering; Food Science; Metals & Metallurgy; Sustainable Energy and Development; Textiles; and others. Knovel's search allows users to find data hidden in tables, graphs, and equations, while numeric range and multivariable search helps them solve complex problems. The My Knovel feature allows users to personalize their research findings.

Business Model: Knovel offers enterprise and academic subscription plans that take into account the size of an organization, its user population, and its information needs. Knovel does not sell individual e-book titles or offer subscriptions to individuals. Pricing for Knovel's enterprise subscription packages begins at $10,000.

LexisNexis Digital Library

Website: www.lexisnexis.com/ebooks/lending
Parent company: LexisNexis
Library markets: academic/research, government, corporate
Platform type: publisher/e-book lending service
E-book type: primary law, deskbooks, legal code books, treatises
Main subjects: law

Background: LexisNexis's unique partnership with OverDrive has led to the 2012 release of LexisNexis Digital Library, a new, publisher-agnostic e-book lending service that offers access to the content of over 1,200 legal e-books on all major mobile devices and desktop platforms. It also enables subscribing organizations to lend individual e-book titles to multiple users, purchase e-books centrally, and manage their titles in one place. The core of LexisNexis Digital Library is a website created by OverDrive that is customized for each law firm or organization (including, for the most part, academic and government law libraries). A librarian (or designated administrator) orders titles and supervises lending of all electronic content via this site. The administrator also generates reports to better understand e-book usage patterns. Legal professionals are able to check out and return titles via the website, via a mobile-optimized version of the site, or through a downloadable mobile application. As a result of the agreement with OverDrive, LexisNexis customers also have access to more than 700,000 titles from OverDrive's Content Reserve collection development portal. LexisNexis e-books are compatible with Windows PC, Mac, iPod, iPhone, iPad, Kindle (US only), Sony eReader, Nook, Android, BlackBerry, and Windows Phone.

Business Model: Individual LexisNexis e-books range in price from $14 to over $1,000, and only select titles are available by subscription. LexisNexis Digital Library pricing varies and ranges from a one user/one copy approach to an unlimited-use pricing model. The librarian who acts as the administrator chooses the length of the checkout period (from 7 to 180 days) and whether books can be renewed.

Literati by Credo

Website: http://literati.credoreference.com
Parent company: Credo Reference
Library markets: academic/research
Platform type: aggregator
E-book type: reference books, encyclopedias, dictionaries, handbooks, almanacs
Main subjects: all

Background: Literati is a research platform that combines Credo's licensed content from over eighty publishers with library-centric technologies. As part of the subscription package, Credo's on-staff librarians and educators partner with each library to support its strategic goals. Literati Topic Pages integrate Credo's reference e-books with a library's existing resources and discovery services and deliver real-time results. Libraries can select the specific journal databases, e-book collections, or news resources they wish to integrate within their Credo's Topic Pages. The Literati team works with the library to embed customized tool tips that help students understand which resource to use for their specific research need. Literati Academic includes 3.4 million reference entries (from about 1,300 titles), more than 550,000 images, audio files, videos, and a growing collection of about 10,000 Topic Pages. Also included is the Mind Map and other embedded tools and services designed to enrich the research experience and integration with course management systems like Blackboard and Moodle. A version of the legacy platform (for academic libraries) is now also available for public and school libraries.

Business Model: Literati is offered on an annual subscription basis. Libraries may opt to enhance their Literati subscription with publisher and subject collections, which are available for perpetual purchase or annual subscription; individual titles from these collections may also be purchased on a title-by-title basis.

MackinVIA

Website: www.mackin.com
Parent company: Mackin Educational Resources
Library markets: K–12, public
Platform type: aggregator
E-book type: reference books, K–12 nonfiction
Main subjects: all

Background: MackinVIA is a web-based portal with over 40,000 e-book titles for use in school and K–12 libraries. The same portal also incorporates forty databases for Pre K–12, many equipped with videos and educator tools. Libraries manage all of their e-books and databases via one login, and the students who use VIA get access to both e-books and databases in one place (but cannot check them out). The content comes from a range of publishers—including ABC-CLIO, Crabtree, Chelsea House, Gale Cengage Learning, Gareth Stevens Publishing, and Rosen—and is accessible through the library's online catalog and/or a link on the school's website. Educators are encouraged to use the platform with interactive boards. Students may search for titles by subject and create VIA groups for grades, classes, reading assignments, etc. Key features include free MARC records and customizable search filters. The platform is expected to grow significantly in 2013.

Business Model: Mackin supports access to single-use e-books, unlimited simultaneous access e-books, and e-book subscriptions. Checked-out titles use lending periods that are established by the system administrator. Libraries purchasing e-books on MackinVIA own them outright and do not need to pay separate annual access fees to keep them on the platform. E-book pricing varies, with most titles falling within the $30–$50 range.

McGraw-Hill eBook Library

Website: http://mhebooklibrary.com
Parent company: McGraw-Hill
Library markets: academic/research, corporate
Platform type: publisher
E-book type: scholarly companions, handbooks, reference books, study aids
Main subjects: business, medicine, engineering, computing

Background: The McGraw-Hill eBook Library includes over 1,400 e-books in the areas of business, medicine, engineering, and computing. There are also fifty collections, each featuring between 15 and 1,250 titles that are grouped under four headings: Engineering and Computing (e.g., civil engineering, consumer computing), Student Study Aids (e.g., AP study guides, school and career exams), Medical (e.g., primary care, nursing, first aid), and Business (e.g., career advice, sales and marketing). Users can sort by title, filter by one of the broad headings, or use the Advanced Search to search by keywords, title, author, ISBN, category, or publication year. Access to the library is web-based, and the e-book displays in the browser. DRM restrictions apply for printing: users can print single pages, with a limit of 10 percent of a title. If they opt to create a login, they can take notes, use bookmarks, and create folders. With the exception of the student study aids, most of the titles are aimed at working professionals.

Business Model: Access is sold on a one-to-four-year subscription basis, with free-of-charge monthly updates and unlimited concurrent usage. Pricing depends on population served for public libraries or FTE for academic institutions. It is possible to purchase individual collections or clusters, but not individual titles. If a library chooses to subscribe to a specific collection for one year, it gets access to existing titles, plus additional frontlist updates that are added to this collection throughout the year.

MyiLibrary

Website: www.myilibrary.com
Parent company: Ingram Content Group
Library markets: academic/research
Platform type: aggregator
E-book type: all
Main subjects: all

Background: With nearly 400,000 titles covering all major disciplines and an additional 5,000 titles added each month, MyiLibrary is one of the fastest-growing e-book platforms available to libraries. It aggregates content from a range of publishers, including Encyclopaedia Britannica, Taylor & Francis, McGraw-Hill, Wiley, Oxford University Press, Cambridge University Press, Springer, and Elsevier. It also provides exclusive access to intergovernmental publications from groups such as the International Atomic Energy Agency, the International Labor Organization, and the World Health Organization. Key features include always-on (remote) access, full-text searching across the entire platform supported by enhanced metadata, and flexible buying options. A variety of secure and controlled access/authentication methods to content is provided using broad DRM implementation. With the acquisition of a title or a collection, a range of user-friendly search options enable users to cross-reference material, view searches in order of relevance, save previous searches, and create bookmarks. The platform is entrenched in the academic/research market, but its presence in public libraries is growing. Major updates are expected in 2013.

Business Model: Ingram's MyiLibrary offers libraries the ability to acquire e-books on a title-by-title basis or to create their own publisher-specific or subject-specific collections, which may be accessed in perpetuity or by subscription. Approval plans are also part of the package.

OverDrive

Website: www.overdrive.com
Parent company: OverDrive
Library markets: public, K–12, academic/research, corporate
Platform type: distributor/e-book lending service
E-book type: trade books, handbooks, reference books, comic books, children's books
Main subjects: all
Background: Founded in 1986 and in the e-book business since 2000, OverDrive is the largest public library

e-book vendor, now offering about 1 million titles from 2,000 publishers on its platform. E-books, audiobooks, and videos are available on the same platform in a variety of fiction and nonfiction genres. OverDrive is the only library vendor that offers direct download to Kindle devices. Its online catalog, Content Reserve, also contains digital books in more than fifty languages, including Russian, Swedish, Portuguese, Italian, and Spanish. OverDrive creates the custom website for each library, provides staff training, and lets librarians set lending policies and periods. A single website is used for browsing, checking out titles, and downloading. In 2012, OverDrive announced a new e-book reading platform, OverDrive Read, which enable readers using standard web browsers to read e-books online and offline without needing to install any software or activate their device. OverDrive is also testing new Media Stations for touchscreen monitors and Internet workstations to help raise visibility of e-books in libraries.

Business Model: Libraries pay a subscription fee based on the number of titles they license (and lend to patrons), which is determined based on the population of the service area. Simultaneous access collections are available on an annual subscription basis and can supplement a library's existing one copy/one user collection. Libraries get to decide on their institution's lending policies. Annual maintenance and hosting fees apply.

Oxford Handbooks Online

Website: www.oxfordhandbooks.com
Parent company: Oxford University Press
Library markets: academic/research
Platform type: publisher
E-book type: handbooks
Main subjects: humanities, social sciences

Background: Oxford Handbooks Online (OHO) houses over 300 handbooks and 10,000 articles in fourteen different disciplines, including archeology, classical studies, business and management, philosophy, music, politics, etc. The platform was significantly revamped in 2012 and relaunched as a publishing "program," enabling articles to publish immediately after passing peer review. Each subject (or discipline) has been assigned an editor-in-chief as well as an editorial board of subject experts, who oversee the publication of handbooks within the program and also commission online-only articles in cutting-edge topics. The relaunch of OHO introduced two main content collections: the Foundation Collection (everything available in print up until the first half of 2012) and the Annual Collections (all new content available within a calendar year, including newly released handbooks, in addition to articles written for future handbooks or for online-only publication). OHO is fully cross-searchable within the Oxford Index, a free discovery service, and it features freely available abstracts and keywords at the handbook and article level.

Business Model: The Foundation Collection is available across fourteen subject areas via perpetual access only and on an unlimited user basis. The Annual Collections are available by either perpetual access or subscription across all fourteen subject areas. Institutions can also choose to subscribe to OHO to gain full access to both collections.

Oxford Reference

Website: www.oxfordreference.com
Parent company: Oxford University Press
Library markets: academic/research, public, K–12
Platform type: publisher
E-book type: dictionaries, companions, encyclopedias
Main subjects: general reference

Background: Oxford Reference is the online home of Oxford University Press's 300-plus reference books, which include subject, language, and quotation dictionaries and a wide variety of companions and encyclopedias. The platform is made up of two fully integrated and cross-searchable collections (linked to the Oxford Index): Oxford Quick Reference is all about quickly checking a fact or finding key information about a concept, person, or term; Oxford Reference Library is all about in-depth research and specialist content. In addition, free content supplements the paid content: researchers can use Oxford Reference without paid access from anywhere (or with limited title access) to start their inquiry. Included are over 2 million entries, twenty-five different subject areas; a variety of English and American dictionaries; bilingual dictionaries in French, German, Spanish, and Italian; over 18,000 illustrations, including color photographs, maps, tables, and more; over 300,000 overview pages; over 275 free time lines linking some 9,000 key historical events; and thousands of weblinks.

Business Model: Oxford Reference Library is available for purchase in perpetuity on a title-by-title basis. Oxford Quick Reference is available by subscription to institutions as well as individuals. Annual platform fees apply if a library is not subscribing to any content or does not take any new content for two years.

Palgrave Connect

Website: www.palgraveconnect.com
Parent company: Palgrave Macmillan
Library markets: academic/research

Platform type: publisher
E-book type: monographs, handbooks, reference works
Main subjects: economics, finance, business, arts, humanities, social sciences

Background: Palgrave Connect offers libraries a site license for Palgrave Macmillan's complete e-book collection or for any number of collections in eleven subject areas: Economics & Finance; Political & International Studies; History; Business & Management; Language & Linguistics; Religion & Philosophy; Social Sciences; Literature; Media & Culture; Education; and Theatre & Performance. The platform brings together backlist (going back to 1997) and new (added monthly) titles and now includes about 11,500 e-books in total. Librarians can choose from about 100 collections, arranged by both publication year and subject. The platform integrates with the library's catalog, and free MARC21 records are provided.

Business Model: Palgrave Connect is sold on a perpetual-ownership basis, with two available models: Collection (choose from 100+ collections) and Build-Your-Own-Collection (pick titles from across subject areas; a minimum twenty-title purchase is required). Access to Palgrave Connect allows simultaneous users concurrent access to all purchased content in perpetuity. Perpetual access is free as long as the subscribing institution maintains an active site license to a frontlist collection.

PsycBOOKS

Website: www.apa.org/pubs/databases/psycbooks
Parent company: American Psychological Association (APA)
Library markets: academic/research
Platform type: publisher
E-book type: scholarly monographs, professional literature
Main subjects: psychology, behavioral sciences

Background: PsycBOOKS provides e-access to the full text of thousands of cross-searchable scholarly and professional books, including recent APA titles in psychological and behavioral science, plus a substantial backfile of historic works. It comprises scholarly publications ranging from the most current clinical theories to the books published in the early seventeenth century, professional titles that present applications for behavioral science in contemporary issues, and chapters from hard-to-find classic books. Access is also provided to the 1,500 entries in the *Encyclopedia of Psychology*, copublished by APA and Oxford University Press. Of the 3,500+ books included, 910 are published by APA and about 100 are out of print. PsycBOOKS does not include APA Style products, Magination Press children's titles, APA LifeTools trade book titles, APA Handbooks in Psychology, textbooks, encyclopedias, or other reference publications. There is a twelve-month embargo on titles before they are made available online.

Business Model: Individual access to PsycBOOKS can be obtained in two ways: via subscription access (PsycBOOKS is included in a subscription to APA PsycNET Gold, APA PsycNET Gold Plus, and APA PsycNET Platinum) or via on-demand access (searching is free, users pay only when they download full-text chapters). Institutional access is provided to libraries via a subscription model directly by the publisher or via several other vendors, including EBSCO, Ovid, and ProQuest. APA offers industry standard terms for site licenses, including remote access, perpetual access, and ILL and electronic course reserves for full text. License fees cover unlimited access for all users affiliated with the institutional licensee.

Questia

Website: www.questia.com
Parent company: Cengage Learning
Library markets: academic/research, grades 9–12
Platform type: aggregator
E-book type: scholarly publications, monographs, reference books, encyclopedias
Main subjects: arts, humanities, social sciences, science, technology, medicine

Background: Questia is an online research and paper-writing resource that was founded in 1998 and acquired by Cengage Learning in 2010. It helps students at high school and college level find and cite scholarly research. Questia combines a library of 76,500 online books and 9 million full-text articles with tools that help students write research papers more efficiently. Topics covered include history, philosophy, economics, political science, English and literature, anthropology, psychology, and sociology, among many others. E-books are fully integrated with journal, magazine, and newspaper articles as well as encyclopedia entries.

Business Model: For high schools, the Questia School product can be purchased on an institutional or district level, with pricing based on the full-time equivalent (FTE) figure and individual accounts then created based on that figure. Within higher education, Questia can be purchased at a discount on an individual student basis when bundled with a Cengage print product or as part of a bulk distribution (with no minimum requirement). For Questia School, a minimum commitment of $750 is required. Individuals may sign up for an annual membership for $99.95, a semester membership for $49.95, or a monthly membership for $19.95.

R2 Digital Library

Website: http://r2library.com
Parent company: Rittenhouse Book Distributors
Library markets: academic/research, professional
Platform type: distributor/aggregator
E-book type: scholarly and professional literature, handbooks
Main subjects: medicine, nursing, health

Background: Launched in 2005, R2 Digital Library is a web-based platform that offers integrated and searchable medical and nursing and allied health book content from fifty health science publishers, including Lippincott Williams & Wilkins, Delmar (Cengage Learning), Elsevier, Springer, Wiley, and the American Academy of Pediatrics. There are over 3,000 e-books on the platform, with more added each month. Key features include customized saved searches, images, references and bookmarks, an A–Z drug index, and an A–Z topic index. Content can be browsed by category, discipline, or title, and users can perform searches across the entire platform. A new version of the RD Digital Library launched in summer of 2012 and included the following enhancements: updated user interface, more faceted search tools, and expanded reading pane. Usage statistics are COUNTER-compliant and can be downloaded, printed, or e-mailed directly from the R2 Digital Library. The platform does not allow direct download of e-books, but the web-based application allows e-books to be accessed at any time. Users are able to print or e-mail portions of the R2 Digital Library by using the Tools icon located on the top navigation bar.

Business Model: R2 Digital Library e-books are sold individually by concurrent user license, allowing libraries to purchase only the titles they want to add to their collection. All e-books are purchased for the life of the edition with a one-time payment. When a new edition is released, libraries obtain access to an old edition via R2 Digital Library Archives. There is an annual $1,200 maintenance fee that covers archiving, image hosting, etc. This fee is waived for the first year of usage and can be paid annually or monthly.

Routledge Reference Online

Website: http://routledgeonline.com
Parent company: Taylor & Francis
Library markets: academic/research
Platform type: publisher
E-book type: encyclopedias, dictionaries, handbooks, companions
Main subjects: arts, humanities, social sciences

Background: Routledge Reference Online provides access to e-book versions of Routledge encyclopedias, dictionaries, handbooks, and companions in nine collections. In late 2011, the publisher added six new subject areas (education, history, literature, media and cultural studies, philosophy, and sociology) to complement the existing collections in music, politics, and religion. Each subject collection is regularly updated with new titles, and there are cross-reference links between all titles. Key features include regularly updated title lists, enabling a library's collection to grow under one subscription; federated search, allowing cross-searching across all subject collections; and COUNTER-compliant usage statistics. The product is expected to undergo a major revision in 2013.

Business Model: Routledge Reference Online is an annual subscription product. Libraries can subscribe to as many subject areas as they like, and subscriptions can begin and end at any time. The cost of an annual subscription varies by size of institution and number of concurrent users (usually running between $600 and $4,000), with options available for unlimited access.

Safari Books Online

Website: www.safaribooksonline.com
Parent company: Safari Books Online LLC
Library markets: academic/research, public
Platform type: aggregator
E-book type: reference books, professional nonfiction
Main subjects: information technology, business, graphic design

Background: In 2001, two technology publishers, O'Reilly Media and Pearson Education, joined forces to create Safari Books Online. The goal was to compile the technology books of the two companies into an online database for technology, IT, and management professionals. Since then, Safari Books Online has grown into an interactive, on-demand e-book platform with embedded tools for finding and managing information by nearly 200 other publishers, among them Wiley, Microsoft Press, Cisco Press, Addison-Wesley, Adobe Press, and many others. Subscribers—including libraries, agencies, and business individuals—get online access to nearly 28,000 books, training videos, rough cuts, and short cuts. Content may be read on a computer or a mobile device, and it can be downloaded, saved, printed, or cached for offline reading. Subscriptions for academic and public libraries are available via ProQuest.

Business Model: The cost varies depending on type and level of subscription. Individual subscribers can choose between Safari Library (the all-you-can-eat model) for $42.99 per month or the ten-slot bookshelf model for $27.99 per month. Workgroups of two to twenty-five members can sign up for a subscription online. The cost for a workgroup subscription is $472.89 per user per year for a library subscription and $299 per user per year for a bookshelf subscription. Enterprises or departments with twenty or more members are eligible for additional discounts. Prices vary depending upon the number of seats and content volume. Pricing is based on the number of concurrent seats and the volume of the content offered.

SAGE Knowledge

Website: http://knowledge.sagepub.com
Parent company: SAGE Publications
Library markets: academic/research, corporate, public
Platform type: publisher
E-book type: reference books, monographs, handbooks, professional development titles
Main subjects: sociology, psychology, education, business, counseling, media communications

Background: SAGE Knowledge is an e-book platform billed as "the ultimate social sciences online library" for students, researchers, and faculty. The platform hosts 2,750 titles, which includes 300+ reference works (with 150 new titles added each year). Researchers can search across scholarly monographs, handbooks, reference books, and professional development titles. All of SAGE's imprints are represented, including CQ Press and Corwin. Since the platform features full-text XML content, books and chapters are also fully searchable. With multiple ways to browse, users can elect to start a search by title, by author, or by subject on the homepage and drill down into select content from there. SAGE's content is categorized into ten subject collections, from Sociology and Geography to Criminology to Health and Social Care. Key features include related content, personalized research, DOIs registered for each title and chapter (deposited in CrossRef), and unlimited simultaneous usage of all titles.

Business Model: The following models are available to libraries: full collection + annual top-ups; book collection + annual top-ups; reference collection + annual top-ups; subject collections + annual top-ups; reference mix-and-match title-by-title; and a subscription option.

ScienceDirect

Website: www.sciencedirect.com
Parent company: Elsevier
Library markets: academic/research
Platform type: publisher
E-book type: monographs, handbooks, textbooks, reference books, professional books
Main subjects: science, technology, medicine

Background: ScienceDirect integrates articles and chapters from more than 2,500 journals and more than 11,000 e-books covering a broad range of scientific disciplines and including those published under the Academic Press and Pergamon imprints. The platform offers search and retrieval functionality and a host of new tools that allow users to access content at an early publication stage; download, store, and print it; or pass it on to colleagues. Since 2003, authors have been able to submit extra value-added content associated with their research, including audio and video files, datasets, and other supplementary content. In one access point, users access all of Elsevier's monographs, series books, handbooks, and reference works, which are fully integrated with journal articles.

Business Model: E-books are available in collections and on a pick-and-choose basis. Libraries may purchase books on ScienceDirect regardless of whether they already have an institutional ScienceDirect agreement. Existing ScienceDirect customers receive an amendment to existing contract agreements. New customers who sign up for only the e-books portion of the platform need to pay an annual maintenance fee of 5 percent of the purchased value. Online-only access to books is purchased separately from print versions. The fee is charged according to the number of full-time equivalents (FTEs) within an institution.

Sharpe Online Reference (SOLR)

Website: http://sharpe-online.com
Parent company: ME Sharpe, Inc.
Library markets: academic/research, public, grades 9–12
Platform type: publisher
E-book type: reference books
Main subjects: social sciences

Background: SOLR offers a multidisciplinary perspective on US and global history and culture and analysis of cultural, social, political, and economic aspects of history from earliest times to the present via nearly thirty multivolume reference books (among them Colonial America and the Encyclopedia of World Trade). Included are thousands of articles and images, along with thousands of bibliographies and weblinks. Content is reviewed and updated annually at no charge to libraries to ensure currency. New titles are also added annually. Supplementary resources include a multimedia primary source archive, Web Links in History, and teachers' resources. Key features include quick search, search within results, multiple search refinements (articles, documents, images, chronologies, and more), topic finder, and image gallery.

Business Model: SOLR titles are available for one-time purchase with no annual fees. Titles can be purchased individually or in cost-saving US or global packages (25 percent discount). The complete collection is further discounted (30 percent). Multiple title discounts are also available: three to five titles (10 percent), six to nine titles (15 percent), and ten+ titles (25 percent). Further discounts apply when print and online are ordered together. Tiered pricing is based on number of schools per district, academic FTE, and public library population served. Purchase price includes extensive supplementary resources including primary source archives and free annual updates.

SpringerLink

Website: http://link.springer.com
Parent company: Springer Science+Business Media
Library markets: academic/research, corporate, government
Platform type: publisher/aggregator
E-book type: reference books, series books, monographs, textbooks
Main subjects: science, technology, medicine

Background: SpringerLink is an integrated full-text database for journals, books, protocols, reference works, and book series by forty publishers. It comprises thousands of peer-reviewed journals and 88,000 e-books (translating to about 6 million research documents). Libraries may opt to purchase Springer Book Archives within the platform, which includes German economics books by Gabler, the US information technology publisher Apress, and the US nonfiction publisher Copernicus Publications. The following subjects are covered, among others: biomedical sciences, business and management, chemistry, energy, engineering, environmental sciences, mathematics, and statistics. Medical books account for the largest share of the book archives, at over 20 percent. All content can be viewed in PDF, and a significant portion of newer content is also available in full-text HTML. The content is accessible on mobile devices. There is no separate mobile site, but the site adapts to each screen appropriately.

Business Model: Springer e-books are offered as an annual package, whereby libraries and institutions can purchase either the entire annual collection or any number of subject collections. Full archiving rights with continuous access to purchased content are free through SpringerLink as long as the subscribing institution's account remains active with Springer.

SpringerReference

Website: http://springerreference.com
Parent company: Springer Science+Business Media
Library markets: academic/research, corporate
Platform type: publisher
E-book type: encyclopedias, handbooks, dictionaries, bibliographies
Main subjects: science, technology, medicine

Background: Designed to keep content current, SpringerReference contains the latest and forthcoming reference works from the SpringerReference program. It is published as a live web resource, with full text made accessible to subscribing institutions. What sets it apart from other scholarly platforms is the feature that allows authors to track and publish changes to their articles or charts in near-real time. Reference books on SpringerReference are complementary to those found on SpringerLink (above). While SpringerLink's reference books are static, SpringerReference's are continually updated. The content is vetted by experts in various disciplines and monitored by an editorial board. The platform also provides researchers with the first look at new reference books before they appear in print or on the SpringerLink platform. There are no DRM restrictions. Individuals have the option to save or print the PDF of an article.

Business Model: SpringerReference is available through two business models: a stand-alone subscription model with an annual, tiered subscription fee or a subscription at a reduced rate in combination with other Springer e-book deals.

StarWalk Kids Media

Website: http://starwalkkids.com
Parent company: Seymour Science LLC
Library markets: K–12, public
Platform type: distributor
E-book type: children's illustrated books and chapter books
Main subjects: YA fiction, science, social studies, language arts

Background: StarWalk Kids Media is a new provider of K–12 e-books (149 at launch, 400 by June 2013) for schools and libraries. Its digital collection delivers e-book titles from a variety of children's book authors and illustrators. Each title has been created for a digital reading experience: children can read for themselves, read along at their own pace accompanied by professional narration, or follow the narration throughout the book for a read-to-me experience. The titles (a mix of fiction and nonfiction) support the Common Core State Standards and are recommended to libraries as alternatives to more expensive platforms. The company's proprietary, browser-based StarWalk Reader software works on any device, including desktop and laptop computers, interactive whiteboards, and tablets with Internet connections. The company is currently in negotiations with several children's book publishers for rights to bring their titles into the platform.

Business Model: The collection is sold by annual subscription for schools and libraries. Streaming access is provided to subscribers anywhere that the user has Internet connectivity. Since this is a streaming, subscription-based platform, StarWalk does not limit the number of users who can access a single title at the same time. Instead a username/password authentication scheme is used, so an entire class with an active subscription can read the same book at the same time without any check-in/check-out restrictions or waiting lists. Subscription plans for institutions start at $595 per year for a single school and are based on cardholder population or FTEs for public and university libraries.

Storia

Website: http://scholastic.com/storia
Parent company: Scholastic, Inc.
Library markets: Pre K–grade 8
Platform type: publisher
E-book type: picture books, transitional chapter books, middle fiction, YA nonfiction
Main subjects: general

Background: Storia is Scholastic's free e-reading app designed to help kids learn in an interactive way. The initial download comes with five free titles, with thousands of additional titles available for purchase. There is also a selection of "enriched" e-books that include learning activities within each story to boost comprehension and reading retention. Other features include "Read-to-Me" audio narration; study tools such as the Highlighter and Note-Taker; and the Storia Dictionary, a customized, age-appropriate dictionary that is embedded into each story. Educators are able to set up personalized bookshelves and assign e-books to each shelf to guarantee a customized experience for every reader. Each bookshelf is also linked to the Reading Reports feature, which allows educators to track reading progress by following metrics such as, for example, the number of e-books opened and words looked up and average Guided Reading or Lexile levels. The app is available for iPad, PC, and select Android tablets, with more platforms on the horizon in and beyond 2013.

Business Model: Storia e-books may be purchased in several ways. Classroom eCollections, discounted bundles of specially selected e-books by grade range, are available for purchase online at www.scholastic.com/storia-classroom or through purchase orders, which may be downloaded on the Scholastic website. Librarians can also purchase e-books individually through the Scholastic Store online or through Scholastic Book Clubs. All Storia e-books ordered through book clubs earn the educator bonus points that can be redeemed for books, e-books, or professional resources. Bulk orders can also be customized on an ad hoc basis.

SwetsWise

Website: http://swets.com/ebooks
Parent company: Swets Information Services
Library markets: academic/research, corporate, government
Platform type: distributor
E-book type: scholarly publications
Main subjects: all

Background: Swets, a division of Swets Information Services, develops content management solutions for libraries, end users, and publishers. SwetsWise, the company's catalog of over 1 million e-books, is updated with new titles and partners continuously. Librarians can use SwetsWise's integrated selection tools to find the best offer (from both publishers and aggregators) and then acquire the titles they want. A single interface is used to select and manage journals and e-books. Full-text access is then provided through the online content delivery platform that the library chooses. Librarians may locate titles using basic and advanced search functionalities, including the option to search on the basis of the print ISBN. SwetsWise also provides a host of optional services for libraries, including an A–Z overview of a library's holdings, allowing patrons to jump to the full text on the platform of choice. In addition, SwetsWise provides a federated search service, allowing patrons to obtain relevant search results from all content delivery platforms from a single interface.

Business Model: Through SwetsWise, librarians can purchase both individual titles and e-book collections under the same pricing and purchase models as offered through the publishers and aggregators directly. Popular acquisition models include pick-and-choose in perpetuity; subject collections in perpetuity; patron-driven collections through aggregators in perpetuity; and annual subscription collections.

Taylor & Francis eBooks

Website: www.tandfebooks.com
Parent company: Taylor & Francis

Library markets: academic/research, corporate, government, public
Platform type: publisher
E-book type: companions, handbooks, monographs, reference books, textbooks
Main subjects: STM, behavioral sciences, humanities, law, social sciences

Background: Live since August 2012, Taylor & Francis's e-book platform brings together academic content of three of its well-known imprints: Routledge, Focal Press, and Psychology Press. The platform currently has over 30,000 e-books covering the humanities, social sciences, behavioral sciences, STM, and law. The collection is due to grow to around 50,000 e-books by the end of 2013. Key features include annotation tools, full-text searching, and unrestricted printing and copy/paste options for 75 percent of e-books; for the 25 percent of the titles with DRM protection, there is a copy/paste allowance of 1,000 words per user session and a print allowance of 30 pages per user session. Users can drill down from content in headline subject areas to titles in specific niche topics and build a short list of relevant titles. Librarians looking for complementary materials to university courses should also consider investing in Taylor & Francis's eFocus packages. These are made up of titles hand-picked by the internal editorial teams and cover, among other topics, the environment, globalization, urban studies, and human rights.

Business Model: A range of flexible purchase options are available for institution access. Librarians may choose to subscribe or purchase content outright, invest in "great-value-for-money" subject collections, or pick and mix individual titles. Libraries that subscribe to the archive and subscription packages gain free access to all of the backlist titles while retaining permanent access to the frontlist titles during the life of the subscription.

TrueFlix

Website: http://trueflix.scholastic.com
Parent company: Scholastic, Inc.
Library markets: grades 3–8, public
Platform type: publisher
E-book type: children's nonfiction
Main subjects: social studies, science

Background: Delivered completely over the Internet, TrueFlix is based on the nonfiction content from Children's Press print book series *True Books*, and its digital backbone is modeled after the BookFlix digital platform. It consists of over eighty e-books and a corresponding number of lesson plans, project ideas, and videos; 1,345+ articles from Grolier Online; 760+ vetted weblinks; 500+ primary sources; and 168 open-ended questions for teachers to use to encourage classroom discussion. Used individually by students or in a classroom with a whiteboard, the platform is designed to teach the inquiry method to younger researchers, and it is fully aligned with Common Core State Standards.

Business Model: Access to the platform may be purchased through Scholastic Library Publishing only. Annual subscription for school and public libraries includes unlimited, 24/7 multiuser simultaneous and remote access from home. Annual platform fees apply for subscriptions. No purchase-to-own option is available.

University Press Scholarship Online (UPSO)

Website: www.universitypressscholarship.com
Parent company: Oxford University Press
Library markets: academic/research
Platform type: university press consortium
E-book type: scholarly monograph
Main subjects: humanities, social sciences

Background: UPSO is a partnership between Oxford University Press and a number of university presses—including Fordham, University of Florida, Stanford University, the American University in Cairo, Edinburgh University, Hong Kong University, and Manchester University—to aggregate monograph content into a single, cross-searchable platform featuring XML. Oxford University Press set the stage for digitization of scholarly monographs in 2003 with the launch of Oxford Scholarship Online, now fully integrated with the monograph content of eleven (and counting) partner presses on the new UPSO platform. The platform offers well over 1,000 titles available in twenty-four subject areas and over 300 subdisciplines. Subjects covered include law, music, physics, religion, biology, philosophy, mathematics, history, and business and management, among others. New, recently published, or not-yet-published-in-print content is added to the platform three times a year: in January, May, and September.

Business Model: UPSO pricing is based on the print list price of the books that an institution buys access to, which increases based on the size of the institution's FTE. UPSO provides a number of content collections available by publisher, by subject area (e.g., history), and/or by subcategory (e.g., nineteenth century American history). All collections are available by perpetual access (giving institutions unlimited use rights) or annual subscription. New university press sites are launched on the platform throughout the year, and title lists for these launches are available six to eight months in advance.

University Publishing Online

Website: http://universitypublishingonline.org
Parent company: Cambridge University Press
Library markets: academic/research, public
Platform type: university press consortium
E-book type: monographs, textbooks, professional books
Main subjects: humanities, social sciences, science and engineering, medicine

Background: The result of a joint venture between Cambridge University Press and partner publishers—including Liverpool University, Mathematical Association of America, University of Adelaide Press, Boydell & Brewer, and others—University Publishing Online integrates scholarly books (including textbooks and professional books) with journal articles on a single platform. The platform offers 22,000 titles covering the strength subjects of the partner presses: anthropology, fine arts, classical studies, computer science, environmental science, education, engineering, performing arts, geography, history, language and linguistics, law, management, mathematics, medicine, philosophy, politics and international relations, and sociology. New titles are added on a monthly basis.

Business Model: Two purchasing plans are available, each involving multiuser concurrent access and minimal DRM. Libraries can purchase predefined subject collections or assemble custom packages. Purchasing plans include a perpetual access model (buy content once and then own continuing access), approval plans, advance ordering, and annual subscription (with a subscribe-to-buy option).

UPCC Book Collections on Project MUSE

Website: http://muse.jhu.edu
Parent company: Johns Hopkins University Press
Library markets: academic/research, public
Platform type: university press consortium
E-book type: monographs, scholarly publications
Main subjects: social sciences, arts, humanities

Background: The University Press Content Consortium (UPCC) brings together over 20,000 e-books from more than eighty university presses and related scholarly publishers, available on the same platform with MUSE's more than 500 scholarly journals. Key features include unlimited simultaneous usage of book content, no DRM or restrictions on printing or downloading, COUNTER-compliant usage statistics, free MARC records, books released electronically simultaneous with print publication, DOIs at title and chapter level, books in chapter-level PDF format, and mobile access to books on any PDF-compatible device. Libraries are able to access information on title availability from various UPCC presses through GOBI3 (Global Online Bibliographic Information), YBP's acquisition and collection management interface. Libraries can elect to receive new title notifications from GOBI3 or have titles automatically delivered by the MUSE platform through YBP's eApproval program.

Business Model: UPCC e-books are available via two subscription options. The Current Subscription option provides access to all UPCC books in MUSE published or due to publish in 2011, 2012, and 2013. The Archival Subscription option provides access to all e-books published prior to 2011. Purchase options for both current and archival collections include complete, subject, area studies, and annual supplemental collections. Individual e-book purchasing will be available in 2013.

Wheelers ePlatform

Website: www.eplatform.co
Parent company: Wheelers Books
Library markets: public, K–12
Platform type: distributor/e-book lending service
E-book type: popular fiction and nonfiction, educational materials
Main subjects: all

Background: This library lending service hosts and facilitates the lending and downloading of e-book titles using the Adobe DRM platform. With over 800 publishers profiled, ePlatform is available in over 500 libraries in ten countries, including Australia, New Zealand, the United Kingdom, South Africa, Ireland, and more recently, the United States. Notable features include free set-up options, no annual fees, and no minimum buying requirements. Other features include flexible administration control over loan parameters (from one to sixty days) and on reserves/holds. Librarians can restrict borrowing of titles by age or year at school, download usage reports, and profile their own digital content from their local community. Libraries can also integrate free e-books from Project Gutenberg into their catalogs for simultaneous use.

Business Model: Wheelers e-books are purchased at the digital list price together with a one-off $2 hosting/DRM fee per e-book. After that there are no annual fees and no minimum purchase requirements. It is therefore possible to set up for free and buy only one title if a library chooses.

Wiley Online Library

Website: http://onlinelibrary.wiley.com
Parent company: John Wiley & Sons, Inc.

Library markets: academic/research
Platform type: publisher
E-book type: scholarly handbooks, companions, professional books, reference books
Main subjects: life, health, and physical sciences; social sciences; humanities

Background: Wiley-Blackwell, the scholarly publishing business of John Wiley & Sons, publishes nearly 1,500 peer-reviewed journals and over 1,500 books annually in print and online. Its online portal, Wiley Online Library (WOL), is a multidisciplinary collection of resources covering the sciences, social sciences, and humanities. The "book" module of WOL, Wiley Online Books (WOB), provides access to over 12,000 scholarly books that are integrated with the journals, hundreds of multivolume reference works, laboratory protocols, and databases via CrossRef, within and outside WOL. The books are available in sixty-seven subject collections, which include titles published through 2011. Notable features include OpenURL with links and DOIs, no DRM restrictions on downloads and printing, COUNTER-compliant usage data, and enhanced MARC Records from OCLC at no extra charge.

Business Model: Wiley books can be added to a library collection in three ways: one-time fee option (pay once for perpetual access to all the books you buy with no further surcharges); an annual flexible subscription (pay an annual fee for one calendar year, subscribe to any title for three consecutive years, qualify for an auto-purchase feature); or Article Select Tokens and pay-per-view (use tokens or pay with credit card to access book chapters for up to twenty-four hours). Tokens may be purchased on a prepaid, deposit account basis, with a minimum purchase of 100.

World Book Web

Website: http://worldbook.com
Parent company: World Book, Inc.
Library markets: public, K–12, academic/research
Platform type: publisher
E-book type: encyclopedias, dictionaries, research guides
Main subjects: all

Background: The World Book Web (WBW) is a complex suite of research tools that includes access to e-books, encyclopedia articles, primary source collections, educator tools, student activities, pictures, and audio and videos. WBW's modules include World Book Web for Schools (which includes products like World Book Kids, World Book Student, and World Book Advanced, with access to over 5,000 full-length e-books), World Book Online for Public Libraries (which includes products like World Book Online Info Finder and World Book Online Reference Center [WBORC]), World Book Classroom (e.g., Social Studies Power, Activity Corner), and specialty sites like World Book Mobile and Academic World Book. Most of the products on WBW include a range of e-books (for all levels and covering a variety of subjects) that are fully integrated with multimedia, primary and secondary source databases, and the World Book Encyclopedia. Key features include computer and web tutorials for the novice researcher, interactive maps and atlases, research tools that include a built-in dictionary, a citation builder, and local and country research guides.

Business Model: Several subscription packages are available for purchasing institutions and include stand-alone and add-on options. A dedicated training website (http://worldbookonline.com/training/index.htm) has been designed to provide a breakdown of all available products and services within the WBW suite.

Chapter 4

E-book Platforms for Libraries

Comparative Overview

Abstract

Chapter 4 of Library Technology Reports *(vol. 49, no. 3) "E-book Platforms for Libraries" consists of four tables. The at-a-glance table lists all fifty-one products featured in the main directory, while three comparative overview tables zoom in on the key features of thirty-five platforms (by vendors who agreed to supply information necessary for inclusion by given deadline). Librarians may use the tables to gain insight into how certain platforms measure up to others in terms of content, technical specifications, functionality, and business models.*

Table 4.1 is an at-a-glance overview of the fifty-one platforms listed in chapter 3. Each is identified by platform type (e.g., aggregator, publisher, distributor) and main library market (e.g., academic/research, public, K–12), and details about the product's website and parent company are also included. The purpose of this table (arranged alphabetically by product name) is to give librarians a bird's-eye view of the types of e-book platforms they can purchase.

Tables 4.2.1, 4.2.2, and 4.2.3 are comparative overviews of thirty-five of the fifty-one e-book platforms listed in table 4.1. The goal here is to give librarians an understanding of each product's size, scope, technical aspects, and purchasing plans. Librarians should note, however, that this information is time-sensitive and that these tables are not the last word on the scope or purchasing options for the products. E-book platforms frequently go through revisions as vendors revise their offerings, in terms of both content and purchasing plans.

The information in the comparative tables was supplied by the vendors who responded to a questionnaire sent to them electronically in November and December 2012. The report was finalized in January 2013. Not all platforms listed in chapter 3 and in table 4.1 are included in the comparative tables owing to one of the following two reasons: the vendor did not respond to the initial request to provide more information, or the vendor responded but requested not to be included in the comparative tables as its product was in the midst of a significant overhaul at the time the report was compiled.

The specifics for each product are in line with the purchasing criteria discussed in chapter 2 and are broken down into four categories: Content, Technical Specifications, Functionality, and Business Model, as these are usually the most pressing issues that come up in conversations with librarians who purchase e-book platforms for their institutions. The abbreviation n/a is used in a number of fields to indicate that a particular column is not applicable to a product or that the information was not available at the time the vendor was contacted.

Table 4.1
At-a-glance overview of fifty-one e-book platforms

Platform	Website	Platform Type	Parent Company
123Library	https://www.123library.org	aggregator/distributor	123Doc Education
3M Cloud Library	http://ebook.3m.com	distributor/e-book lending service	3M
ABC-CLIO eBook Collection	http://ebooks.abc-clio.com	publisher	ABC-CLIO
Axis 360	http://btol.com/axis360	distributor	Baker & Taylor
Books24x7	www.books24x7.com	aggregator	Skillsoft
Books at JSTOR	http://books.jstor.org	university press consortium	ITHAKA
Books@Ovid	http://site.ovid.com/site/products/books_landing.jsp	aggregator/distributor	Ovid Technologies
Brain Hive	www.brainhive.com	distributor/e-book lending service	Brain Hive
Cambridge Books Online	http://ebooks.cambridge.org	publisher	Cambridge University Press
dawsonera	http://dawsonera.com	distributor	Dawson Books
De Gruyter Online	www.degruyter.com	publisher	De Gruyter
EBL (Ebook Library)	www.eblib.com	e-book lending service	ProQuest
eBooks on EBSCOhost	http://ebscohost.com/ebooks	aggregator	EBSCO Publishing
ebrary	www.ebrary.com	aggregator	ProQuest
epointbooks.com	www.epointbooks.com	publisher	Rosen Publishing
Follett eBooks	http://aboutfollettebooks.com	distributor/e-book lending service	Follet Corporation
Freading Ebook Service	http://freading.com	distributor/e-book lending service	Library Ideas
FreedomFlix	http://freedomflix.digital.scholastic.com/home	publisher	Scholastic
GVRL	www.gale.cengage.com/gvrl	aggregator	Gale Cengage
Infobase eBooks	http://infobasepublishing.com/ebooks	publisher	Infobase Publishing
Knovel	http://why.knovel.com	aggregator	Knovel Corporation
LexisNexis Digital Library	www.lexisnexis.com/ebooks/lending	e-book lending service	LexisNexis
Literati by Credo	http://literati.credoreference.com	aggregator	Credo Reference
MackinVIA	www.mackin.com/via	aggregator	Mackin Educational Resources
McGraw-Hill eBook Library	http://mhebooklibrary.com	publisher	McGraw-Hill
MyiLibrary	www.myilibrary.com	aggregator	Ingram Content Group
OverDrive	www.overdrive.com	distributor/e-book lending service	OverDrive
Oxford Handbooks Online	www.oxfordhandbooks.com	publisher	Oxford University Press
Oxford Reference	www.oxfordreference.com	publisher	Oxford University Press
Palgrave Connect	www.palgraveconnect.com	publisher	Palgrave MacMillan
PsycBOOKS	www.apa.org/pubs/databases/psycbooks	publisher	American Psychological Association
Questia	www.questia.com	aggregator	Cengage Learning
R2 Digital Library	http://r2library.com	aggregator/distributor	Rittenhouse Book Distributors
Routledge Reference Online	http://routledgeonline.com	publisher	Taylor & Francis
Safari Books Online	www.safaribooksonline.com	aggregator	Safari Books Online
SAGE Knowledge	http://knowledge.sagepub.com	publisher	SAGE Publications
ScienceDirect	www.sciencedirect.com	publisher	Elsevier
SOLR	http://sharpe-online.com	publisher	ME Sharpe
SpringerLink	http://link.springer.com	publisher	Springer Science+Business Media
SpringerReference	http://springerreference.com	publisher	Springer Science+Business Media
StarWalk Kids Media	http://starwalkkids.com	distributor	Seymour Science
Storia	http://scholastic.com/storia	publisher	Scholastic
SwetsWise	http://swets.com/ebooks	distributor	Swets Information Services
Taylor & Francis eBooks	www.tandfebooks.com	publisher	Taylor & Francis
TrueFlix	http://trueflix.scholastic.com	publisher	Scholastic
University Press Scholarship Online	www.universitypressscholarship.com	university press consortium	Oxford University Press
University Publishing Online	http://universitypublishingonline.org	university press consortium	Cambridge University Press
UPCC Book Collections on Project MUSE	http://muse.jhu.edu	university press consortium	Johns Hopkins University Press
Wheelers ePlatform	www.eplatform.co	distributor/e-book lending service	Wheelers Books
Wiley Online Library	http://onlinelibrary.wiley.com	publisher	John Wiley & Sons, Inc.
World Book Web	http://worldbook.com	publisher	World Book, Inc.

Table 4.2.1
Comparative overview of thirty-five e-book platforms—content and technical specifications

E-book platform	Main library market	Content				Technical specifications				
		# of e-books	# of publishers	Other content types	Multimedia	Browsers supported	Software or plugins needed	E-book file format	Compatible devices	
3M Cloud Library	public	250,000+	300+	no	no	application-based	3M apps	PDF, ePub	iOS devices, Sony eReader, Nook, most ePub-compatible readers	
Axis 360	public	400,000	300	no	yes (audiobooks, videos)	all	Blio, Adobe Digital Editions or Bluefire Reader; Acoustik (for audiobooks)	PDF, ePub, xps (Blio), Acoustik	iOS devices, Nook, Sony eReader, Kobo	
Books24x7	academic/research	34,000+	845	no	yes (videos)	IE, Safari, Firefox, Chrome	none	HTML, PDF	any tablet or mobile device	
Brain Hive	K–12	3,500	20	no	forthcoming in Fall 2013	all	none	PDF, ePub	iPad	
Cambridge Books Online	academic/research, public	20,000	1	no	no	IE, Safari, Firefox, Chrome, Opera	none	PDF	most	
EBL (Ebook Library)	academic/research	325,000+	500	yes (a small number of journals)	no	all	Adobe Digital Editions	PDF, ePub	any that supports Adobe Digital Editions & Bluefire Reader	
eBooks on EBSCOhost	academic/research, public	350,000	1,400	no	no	all	Adobe Digital Editions, Adobe PDF plugin (for Mac)	PDF	iOS devices, Sony eReader, Nook,	
ebrary	academic/research, public	450,000	500	no	no	IE, Safari, Firefox	Adobe Digital Editions, Java, enabling of cookies & popups required	PDF	Kobo, Nook, Kindle Fire, iPad, Sony eReader	
Follett eBooks	K–12, public	145,000+	1,000 (publisher imprints)	yes (databases)	yes (audiobooks)	IE, Safari, Firefox, Chrome	Adobe Flash Player	proprietary	iPad, Android tablets, Kindle Fire, Nook Color	
Freading Ebook Service	public	50,000	60	no	yes	all	Adobe Digital Editions	PDF, ePub	Nook, iPad, Kobo, Sony eReader, Kindle Fire, Android tablets	
FreedomFlix	K–12, public	40	1	yes (related articles)	yes (videos, slideshows, images)	all	n/a	n/a	all hand-held devices	
Gale Virtual Reference Library	academic/research, public	8,000+	80+	no	no	all	none	PDF, HTML	all major Android & iOS devices	

Table 4.2.1 cont'd

E-book platform	Main library market	Content				Technical specifications			
		# of e-books	# of publishers	Other content types	Multimedia	Browsers supported	Software or plugins needed	E-book file format	Compatible devices
Infobase eBooks	K–12, public, academic/research	4,000	1	no	no	all	Adobe Reader	PDF, HTML, ePub (for some, not all titles)	most devices that have a web browser
Literati by Credo	academic/research, public	1,300	80+	no	yes (images, audio, videos, maps)	all	JavaScript, Adobe Flash, MP3 players	HTML (files may be saved in PDF)	n/a
MackinVIA	K–12, public	100,000	80	yes (databases)	yes (videos)	all	Adobe Digital Editions	proprietary	VIA reader, iPad, Android tablets, Kindle Fire
MyiLibrary	academic/research	400,000	1,450	no	no	all	Adobe Digital Editions (for offline download)	PDF, ePub	Nook, Apple devices, Kindle, Sony eReader
OverDrive	public, K–12, academic/research, corporate	1 million	2,000	no	yes (audiobooks, music, videos)	all	Adobe Digital Editions, OverDrive Media Console app, modern web browser with JavaScript enabled	ePub, PDF, Kindle	all (including Kindle)
Oxford Handbooks Online	academic/research	325+	1	no	yes (videos)	IE, Firefox, Chrome, Opera, Safari	none	XML	forthcoming
Oxford Reference	academic/research, public		300+	no	yes (videos)	all but IE 7 & older	none	XML	forthcoming
Palgrave Connect	academic/research	11,500	1	yes (journals)	no	all	Adobe Reader	PDF for all; ePub for books published in 2011 & beyond	all
PsycBOOKS	academic/research	3,500+	1	yes (articles, databases)	yes (videos)	all	none	PDF	n/a
Questia	academic/research, 9–12	76,500	500	yes (journal, magazine, & newspaper articles)	yes (videos)	all	none	HTML	iPad, iPhone, tablet
Safari Books Online	academic/research	28,000	200	yes (related articles)	yes (videos)	all	Flash (version 10 & up)	PDF	all iOS 3+ devices; all Android 1.5+, 2.1+, Blackberry 6 PlayBook
SAGE Knowledge	academic/research, corporate, public	2,700+	1	yes (journals)	yes (images, videos)	all	Java	PDF, HTML	forthcoming in 2013

Table 4.2.1 cont'd

E-book platform	Main library market	Content				Technical specifications			
		# of e-books	# of publishers	Other content types	Multimedia	Browsers supported	Software or plugins needed	E-book file format	Compatible devices
Sharpe Online Reference	academic/research, public	29 (multivolume)	1	no	yes (audio & video)	all	Java & Flash	HTML	iPad forthcoming
SpringerLink	academic/research	88,000	40+	yes (journals, protocols)	yes (videos)	all	none	PDF, HTML	all
SpringerReference	academic/research	195+	1	no	no	all	none	PDF, HTML	does not support mobile screen size
StarWalk Kids Media	K–12, public	400 (by June 2013)	1	no	yes	IE, Safari, Firefox, Chrome	Flash plugin	PDF, streaming delivery	Nook, iPad, Kindle Fire, iPhone, Android phones
Storia	Pre K–grade 8	3,500	21	no	yes	application-based	Storia app	n/a	iPad, Android tablets
Taylor & Francis eBooks	academic/research, corporate, government, public	35,000+	1	no	no	all	FileOpen plugin	PDF	not yet supported
TrueFlix	K–12, public	84	1	yes (related articles)	yes (videos, slideshows, images)	all	Flash	n/a	all Flash-based devices (by Aug. 2013, non-Flash-based devices will be supported)
University Press Scholarship Online	academic/research	11,200+	11	no	yes (videos)	all	none	XML (printable & downloadable in PDF at chapter level)	all smartphones & tablet devices
University Publishing Online	academic/research	22,000	9	yes (journals)	no	IE, Safari, Firefox, Chrome, Opera	none	PDF	most
UPCC Book Collections on Project MUSE	academic/research; public	20,000+	80+	yes (journals)	no	IE, Firefox, Chrome, Opera	none	PDF	all PDF-compatible
Wheelers ePlatform	public, K–12	100,000	700+	no	no	all	Adobe Digital Editions; Bluefire reading app	PDF, ePub	Nook, iPad, Sony eReader, Samsung Galaxy, Kobo, Android tablets

Table 4.2.2
Comparative overview of thirty-five e-book platforms—functionality

E-book Platform	Full-text searching	Copy/paste	Printing	Offline reading	ADA compliance	Annotation tools	Usage reports	MARC records	Persistent URLs
3M Cloud Library	yes	no	no	yes	no (forthcoming)	yes	no	yes (free)	no
Axis 360	yes	yes (if publisher allows)	yes (if publisher allows)	yes	yes	yes	yes	yes (free)	yes (book level)
Books24x7	yes	yes	yes	no	yes	yes	yes	yes (free)	yes (book level)
Brain Hive	yes	no	no	no	no	no	yes	yes (free)	yes (book level)
Cambridge Books Online	yes	yes	yes	yes	yes	yes	yes	yes (free)	yes (book & chapter level)
EBL (Ebook Library)	yes	yes (up to 5% of any book's content)	yes (up to 20% of any book's content)	yes	yes	yes	yes	yes	yes (book & chapter level)
eBooks on EBSCOhost	yes (for 90% of titles)	yes (for 90% of titles)	yes	yes	yes	yes	yes (free)	yes (book, chapter, & page level)	yes
ebrary	yes	yes	yes	yes	yes	yes	yes	yes (on demand)	yes (collection, book & chapter level)
Follett eBooks	yes	yes (if publisher allows)	yes (if publisher allows)	yes	yes	no	yes	yes	yes (book level)
Freading Ebook Service	no	n/a	n/a	yes	yes	n/a	yes	no	n/a
FreedomFlix	yes	yes	no	no	yes	yes	yes	yes (free)	yes
Gale Virtual Reference Library	yes	yes	yes	yes	yes	no	yes	yes (free)	yes
Infobase eBooks	yes	yes	yes	yes	no	yes	yes	yes (free)	yes (book & chapter level)
Literati by Credo	yes	yes	yes	yes (by saving in PDF)	yes	no	yes	yes (free)	yes (book level, entry, image, topic)
MackinVIA	yes (within VIA reader)	yes (if publisher allows)	yes (if publisher allows)	yes (via MackinVIA app)	n/a	yes	yes	yes (free)	yes (book level)
MyiLibrary	yes	yes	yes	yes	yes	yes	yes	yes	yes (book level)
OverDrive	yes (for OverDrive Read only)	yes (if publisher allows)	yes (if publisher allows)	yes	yes	yes	yes	yes (paid & free options)	yes (to OverDrive Read titles)
Oxford Handbooks Online	yes	yes	yes (in PDF)	no	yes	forthcoming	yes	yes (free)	yes (book & article level)
Oxford Reference	yes	yes	yes (in PDF)	no	yes	forthcoming	yes	yes (free)	yes (all levels)

E-book Platforms for Libraries **Mirela Roncevic**

Table 4.2.2 cont'd

E-book Platform	Full-text searching	Copy/paste	Printing	Offline reading	ADA compliance	Annotation tools	Usage reports	MARC records	Persistent URLs
Palgrave Connect	yes	yes	yes	yes	no	no	yes	yes (free)	yes (book level; chapter level forthcoming)
PsycBOOKS	yes	yes	yes	yes	yes	no	yes	yes	yes
Questia	yes	yes (portions of the content)	yes (one page at a time)	no	yes	yes	no	no	yes (book level)
Safari Books Online	yes	yes	yes	no for libraries; yes for corporate & consumer accounts	yes	yes	yes	yes	yes (book level)
SAGE Knowledge	yes	yes	yes	yes	yes	yes	yes	yes	yes
Sharpe Online Reference	yes	yes (content & images)	yes	no	no	yes	yes	yes (free if requested)	yes (book & chapter level, image)
SpringerLink	yes	yes	yes	yes	yes	no	yes	yes	yes (book & chapter level)
SpringerReference	yes	yes	yes (in PDF)	no	no	no	yes	yes	yes (book & chapter level)
StarWalk Kids Media	yes	yes	no	no	no	no	yes	no	no
Storia	no	no	no	yes	yes	yes	no	no	n/a
Taylor & Francis eBooks	yes	yes	yes	yes	forthcoming in 2013	yes	yes	yes (free)	yes (book level)
TrueFlix	no	yes	no	no	yes	no	yes	yes	yes
University Press Scholarship Online	yes	yes	yes (in PDF)	no	yes	forthcoming	yes	yes (free)	yes (book & chapter level)
University Publishing Online	yes	yes	yes	yes	yes	no	yes	yes (free)	yes (book & chapter level)
UPCC Book Collections on Project MUSE	yes	yes	yes	yes	yes	yes	yes	yes (free)	yes (book & chapter level)
Wheelers ePlatform	no	no	no	yes	no	yes	yes	yes	n/a

Table 4.2.3
Comparative overview of thirty-five e-book platforms—business model details

E-book platform	One user/ one book	Purchase to own	Subscription	Short-term loans	PDA	Annual fee	Minimum commitment	Inter-library loan	Invoicing intervals	Consortial purchasing	Embargo	DRM	Free trials
3M Cloud Library	yes	no	no (in development)	no	yes	no	no	no	monthly	yes	no	full DRM protection	no
Axis 360	yes	yes (single user or multiuser)	no (in development)	no (in development)	no (in development)	yes (for perpetual access)	$1,000 minimum opening order (scaled by size of library)	no	yearly	yes (limitations apply)	mostly no	limited copy/paste & printing	n/a
Books24x7	no	no (but available as an option within the subscription package)	yes	no	no	no	no	no	yearly	yes	no	none	yes
Brain Hive	yes (on demand, rental)	yes	no	yes	yes	no	no	no	monthly	yes	no	full DRM protection	no
Cambridge Books Online	no	no (but available upon request)	yes	forthcoming	no	yes (for perpetual access only)	25 titles	no	vary	yes	yes (4–6 weeks)	minimal	yes (30 days)
EBL (Ebook Library)	no	yes (unlimited, multiuser)	no	yes	yes	yes (nominal)	no	no	weekly & monthly	yes	no	some restrictions apply	yes (30 days)
eBooks on EBSCOhost	yes	yes	yes	yes	yes	no	no	yes	depends on type of purchase	yes (limitations apply)	set by publisher	Adobe DRM applies	yes
ebrary	yes (for perpetual purchases)	yes (unlimited, multiuser)	yes	yes	yes	yes (for perpetual access only)	no (pledges may be required for PDA accounts)	no	yearly (for subscription) & weekly (for PDA)	yes	no	some restrictions apply	yes (30 days)
Follett eBooks	yes	yes	no	no	no	no	no	no	vary	n/a	no	restrictions set by publishers	yes
Freading Ebook Service	yes	no	yes (via tokens)	no	no	no	no	no	vary	n/a	varies; set by publishers	standard DRM	n/a
FreedomFlix	no	no	yes	no	no	yes	no	no	yearly	yes	no	n/a	yes (60 days)

E-book Platforms for Libraries   Mirela Roncevic

Table 4.2.3 cont'd

E-book platform	One user/one book	Purchase to own	Subscription	Short-term loans	PDA	Annual fee	Minimum commitment	Interlibrary loan	Invoicing intervals	Consortial purchasing	Embargo	DRM	Free trials
Gale Virtual Reference Library	no	yes (unlimited, perpetual)	no	no	no	yes	no	no	upon availability of content	yes	no	none	yes (1–4 weeks)
Infobase eBooks	no	yes (unlimited)	yes	no	no	no	no	no	yearly	yes	no	none	yes (30 days)
Literati by Credo	no	yes (for collections)	yes	no	no	no	no	yes	yearly	yes	no	none	no (3-month paid trials only)
MackinVIA	no	yes (unlimited, multiuser)	no	yes (if enabled by administrator)	no	no	n/a	n/a	vary	yes	n/a	none	yes (15–30 days)
MyiLibrary	yes	yes (multiuser, perpetual)	yes	yes	yes	yes (for perpetual access only)	no	yes	n/a	yes	n/a	evaluated on a per-title basis	yes (30 days)
OverDrive	yes (simultaneous & metered access)	no	yes	no	no	yes	no	no	monthly	yes	varies; set by publishers	standard DRM for ePub & WMA	yes
Oxford Handbooks Online	no	yes (unlimited)	yes	no	no	yes (for perpetual access)	no	no	yearly	yes	no	none	yes (30 days)
Oxford Reference	no	yes	yes	no	no	yes	no	no	yearly	yes	no	none	yes (30 days)
Palgrave Connect	no	yes (perpetual)	no	no	no	yes (waived when a current collection is purchased)	20-title minimum for Build-Your-Own model	yes	yearly	yes	no	none	yes (30 & 60 days)
PsycBOOKS	no	no	yes	no	no	yes	n/a	yes (in accordance with license terms)	yearly	yes	yes (12 months)	n/a	yes (30 days)
Questia	no	no	yes	no	no	n/a	$750 for schools; no minimum for higher ed when bundled with a Cengage print product	no	yearly for school; vary for higher ed (monthly, quarterly, yearly, bi-annual)	yes (case-by-case)	no	some restrictions apply	yes (1 day for individuals; 30 days for schools)

E-book Platforms for Libraries **Mirela Roncevic**

Table 4.2.3 cont'd

E-book platform	One user/ one book	Purchase to own	Subscription	Short-term loans	PDA	Annual fee	Minimum commitment	Inter-library loan	Invoicing intervals	Consortial purchasing	Embargo	DRM	Free trials
Safari Books Online	no	no	yes	no	no	no	no	no	yearly (negotiable)	yes	no	n/a	yes (30 days)
SAGE Knowledge	no	no	yes	no	no	no	no	no	yearly	yes	no	none	yes (30 days)
Sharpe Online Reference	no	yes (unlimited)	no	no	no	no	no	no	n/a	yes	no	none	yes (30 days)
SpringerLink	no	yes (perpetual)	no	no	no	yes	no	yes	vary	yes	no	none	yes (up to 90 days)
SpringerReference	no	no	yes	no	no	yes	no	yes	yearly	yes	no	none	yes (60 days)
StarWalk Kids Media	no	no	yes	no	no	no	$595 for schools	no	yearly	yes	no	none	yes (30 days)
Storia	yes	yes	no	no	no	no	no	n/a	vary	negotiable on a case-by-case basis	n/a	yes	n/a
Taylor & Francis eBooks	yes	yes (multiuser & unlimited)	yes	no	no	yes (nominal)	50-title minimum purchase or subscription	no	yearly	yes	no	75% of the catalog is DRM-free	yes
TrueFlix	no	no	yes	no	no	yes	no	no	yearly	yes	no	n/a	yes (60 days)
University Press Scholarship Online	no	yes (unlimited)	yes	no	no	yes (for perpetual access)	no	no	yearly	yes	no	download limited to 5 chapters per session	yes (30 days)
University Publishing Online	no	not standard but available upon request (via perpetual access)	yes	forthcoming	no	yes (for perpetual access only)	25	no	vary	yes	no	minimal	yes (30 days)
UPCC Book Collections on Project MUSE	no	yes (unlimited)	yes	no	no	no	no	yes for owned; no for subscriptions	yearly	yes	no	none	no
Wheelers ePlatform	yes	yes	no	yes	some	no	no	no	monthly	yes	n/a	Adobe DRM applies	yes (30 days)

E-book Platforms for Libraries **Mirela Roncevic**

Notes

Keep up with
Library Technology
REPORTS

	Upcoming Issues
May/June 49:4	**Using Google Analytics: Six High-Priority Projects for Libraries** by Tabatha Farney and Nina McHale
July 49:5	**The Changing Library Metadata Landscape** by Erik T. Mitchell
August/ September 49:6	**The Mobile Web** by Bohyun Kim

Subscribe
alatechsource.org/subscribe

Purchase single copies in the ALA Store
alastore.ala.org

alatechsource.org

ALA TechSource, a unit of the publishing department of the American Library Association

www.ingramcontent.com/pod-product-compliance
Lightning Source LLC
Chambersburg PA
CBHW080925300426
44115CB00018B/2947